Life Adopted

Life Adopted

A search for answers that only God could give

Amy R. Jones

Printed/published by Amy R. Jones in the United States of America

ISBN 979-8-9913477-0-9
First printing 2024

This work depicts events in the author's life. All persons within are actual individuals; there are no composite characters. The names and of some individuals have been changed to respect their privacy.

Dedication

For Mom and Dad

who loved me unconditionally

and introduced me to Jesus.

I'll love you forever

For my birth mother

who decided my life was worth nine months of hers

and loved me enough to give me away

For my daughters

I loved you from the moment you were

and I'll love you even after I'm not

Table of Contents

Preface

"Is this all there is?" The question that started as a gentle tap eventually stomped around screaming, knocking every other thought off the shelf in my mind. My purpose in life felt elusive. I had all the things we hear will make us happy: money, multiple homes, fancy cars, pretty clothes, all the things that a successful real estate career can provide. Yet, nothing satisfied. There had to be more. This overwhelming sense that there was something I was supposed to be doing had nothing to do with money or success. To everyone around me, it looked like I was living my best life, as the saying goes. So why was I so miserable? I've always been a "fixer," but I had no remedy for what I was feeling. I prayed for an answer so often I felt like a nag.

One day, coming to the end of myself, I pray again, "God, where are You? Why aren't You answering me? I feel like there's something You want me to do, but I can't hear You."

And that's when I hear Him. Well, maybe "hear" is the wrong word. It's not a booming voice from the clouds like in the movies. In fact, I don't hear anything at all. I feel the words running through my body like an electrical current.

"Tell your story."

My heart pounding, the words flow through me again as if to confirm it wasn't my imagination.

"Tell your story."

I know the story I'm supposed to tell—the story of my adoption and the search for my birth parents that turned into so much more. A journey that will ultimately become a journey of faith. So here it is, my story. No, that's not right—Here it is, God's story—the story He wrote just for me so I could tell it to you.

Introduction

Adopt: To take by choice into a relationship.

Adopted: Legally made the son or daughter of someone other than a biological parent.

I'm not sure why the word *adopted* held so much power over me. Perhaps if I had considered it a singular event, like being born, I might have felt differently. Instead, adopted became something I was, a part of my identity like a label tattooed on the back of my neck. But even with that label firmly attached, I never thought of the two most important people in my life as my adoptive parents. They were always Mom and Dad, and just like the dimple in my cheek, they were always there. I felt as much a part of them as I would have if I'd shared their DNA.

Adopted was a word that seemed ever-present when I was growing up. People often felt the need to use it when talking about us, the *adopted* child and her *adoptive* parents. The extra word to describe us felt like sandpaper on my soul, an unnecessary descriptor that only reminded me we weren't actually related like they were almost my parents, but not quite. A disclaimer on my identity and theirs. Why did so many feel an extra word was needed to describe our simple parent/child relationship, even if they got it wrong? When *stepparents* or *stepchild* were used, it felt even worse and required a hand-on-my-hips stance to accompany my response, "They're not my stepparents. Stepparents happen when someone becomes your parent only because of the person they're married to, not because they really want to." How often does someone have two stepparents, anyway?

Then there were the recurrent questions, "Have you ever thought about finding your *real* parents?" Or "Do you know who your *natural* parents are?" My response was always the same, *<insert snarky tone here>* "I live with my real parents; they're not missing, nor are they unnatural in any way." End of conversation. I want to apologize today to all those I responded to in that way. I apologize for the words, the tone, and the stink-eye thrown in for good measure. It was my issue, not yours.

For clarification, when you read the words *mom, dad,* or *parents* within these pages, I'm almost always referring to my true mom and dad—the ones who adopted me at birth and loved me every minute after. We share a bond that is much stronger than DNA. Every memory, every milestone, every tear, and every joy, from my first breath until their last, I've shared with them, the parents God gave me. Our bond has never been broken. Not even death could dissolve it.

All that being said, the fact that I was adopted will forever be a part of me, like a physical attribute: brown hair, blue eyes, adopted. Even my puffy yellow baby book, with blanks meticulously filled in by Mom, bears the title "An Adopted Child's Memory Book." The heartwarming tale of being chosen is indeed beautiful, so how could anyone comprehend my deepest desire to simply be acknowledged as theirs, with no need of an adjective? In a world where everyone strives to stand out, all I ever wanted to do was fit in.

I loved it when someone said, "You look just like your dad." My heart swelled with delight and we all smiled and nodded our heads. Dad would wink at me and I'd wink back. It's true. I did look like Dad, and I liked it and I think he liked it, too. But in the end, we all knew the truth. It was just a coincidence. There are plenty of other differences too. I'm tall; my parents were short. By the time I was twelve years old, I towered over them and looked like a giant standing next to them in family photos.

I also had a chubby phase, and my entire family was thin. I learned to use this to my advantage by perfecting a pretty good comedy routine. When someone said, "Amy, do Fat Albert," I'd oblige, using my deep voice, "Hey, hey, hey, it's Fat Albert!" The impersonation was impressive, complete with requisite arm waving and waddle. Everyone laughed, and I sure loved that laughter that signified approval. I hoped they were laughing at my impersonation and not my body, but deep down, I knew my act wouldn't be nearly as funny if

I were skinny. On that note, words alone cannot convey how much I hated shopping for school clothes. Passing all the cute clothes to shop under the “Husky Girls” sign was pure torture. Now please don’t think I was a chubby kid because of some emotional, adoption-driven, psychological eating disorder. No. I was a chubby kid because I could eat nine pieces of French toast in a single sitting and because macaroni and cheese, grilled cheese, and, well, anything with cheese were my favorite lunches. Chocolate milk complimented meals nicely, followed by a Hostess cupcake, fruit pie, or Suzi Q for dessert.

My family was gregarious and loud, and large family gatherings were considered fun for some reason. I learned how to act just like them and developed a wicked sense of humor with a side of sarcasm because my family loved to laugh and did it a lot. They didn’t know that I really preferred being alone with my books. It had nothing to do with not loving them or not wanting to be around them, but all of them at one time? Overwhelming. As far as I know, I’m the only introvert in my family, and I’ve never grown out of it if that’s even possible to do. So in the event I come up missing at a large social gathering, you may find me alone in an empty room, where I’m probably sitting in the quiet, breathing slowly with my eyes closed. After six decades, I don’t think this is something that will ever change for me, and I don’t think there’s anything wrong with it either. I mean, just think how loud the world would be without us introverts. I've been blessed to know a few fellow introverts over the years, or maybe more than a few. It's hard to know for sure since we're so good at faking it around people, putting on our extravert costume when necessary. but longing to return home where the quiet embraces us. I'm thankful that my husband understands me and doesn't get upset when I ask, "Do we really have to go?" Which is usually followed by, "Please don't talk to me, I'm exhausted" after we do.

Another thing about being adopted is medical history or rather the lack of one. "Adopted" should have been stamped on my medical chart. In other words, don't bother asking about family medical history. There isn't one. Like patient zero, I figured my medical history starts with me and, for future generations looking back, it ends with me. It is what it is, as they say.

Lest you think I spent my childhood bemoaning a title I'd been given like some oversensitive crybaby, let me clear that up right now. My feelings about all that accompanied the "adopted" label were nothing more than an irritant when they presented themselves. There is no other life I would rather have had, and that includes a life where my birth mother kept me or any version where she comes back to claim me. In fact, I was actually a little terrified of that last scenario. It was a nightmare born when I was six and my best friend, Maria, spent the night at my house.

Maria was two years older than me and the youngest of seven children. She lived in a small three-bedroom house across the street from my own. Her house was exciting to me, a noisy, chaotic environment filled with children who seemed to have no rules, which was the opposite of my home. We could jump on beds piled high with clothes and eat cookies without sitting at the kitchen table. Maria didn't have any toys, as far as I could tell, so I was excited to give her a new doll for her birthday. The following day, that doll was hanging on her living room wall like a piece of art, box and all, right next to a framed picture of the Virgin Mary. As far as I know, that doll in the box hung there until the day they moved away. Maria never got to play with it, and I never understood why. When I asked her, she just shrugged and didn't seem bothered by it at all.

Most of the time, Maria and I played at my house, a.k.a. the house of toys, even though we had to sit at the kitchen table to eat cookies and well—anything, and jumping on beds was never allowed. During one of Maria's many sleepovers and at the end of our bedtime prayers, she adds, "And God, please let me swap lives with Amy. Amen."

My eyes spring open in panic as I imagine her prayer floating up to God. Squeezing my eyes shut, I silently pray, "Dear God, pay no attention to what Maria just said."

With that single prayer, my fear is born. A fear that my place in my home and with my family may not be secure. This eventually turned into a fear that my birth mother might show up to take me back, until it is one day replaced with a question that seems to hum in the background of my mind, like an electrical current, "*Who am I, and why didn't my birth mother want me?*" No matter how much I loved and was loved by my family, the questions about my origins would not be quieted.

This is the story of my search for answers to those questions and so much more. It's a journey that spans over thirty-five years and is filled with twists, turns, roadblocks, and so many miracles that it feels made up. I assure you it is not.

mom, dad and me

Memories

What is your very first memory? When you dive into the deep well of your earliest experiences, what do you find? I've asked many friends this question, and we usually find a common denominator. The very first memories are usually so random that one could argue they're not worth much.

My first memory takes place at floor level through my eyes as I crawl down the hallway in my childhood home. I'm heading towards the kitchen when I hear someone calling out, "Boo!" I crawl towards that voice as I yip, "Boo!" in response. Arriving at my apparent destination beneath the kitchen table, I turn from crawling and plant my rear on a red, white, and black crocheted rag rug. Looking under the kitchen table, I see them. Puffy ankles stuffed into black lace-up lady shoes. The crossed ankles are attached to equally puffy legs, with a printed cotton dress covering the knees. The person all of this belongs to is sitting at the table next to the radiator.

That's it. Nothing extraordinary. When I share this memory with Mom, she says, "That was Ma. Hard to believe you'd remember that, but that's what she wore and where she always sat at the table. We taught you to yell 'boo' whenever we yelled it so we'd know where you were in the house." The very first tracking device, no batteries required.

"Ma" was Grandma Amy, my namesake, who lived with us. She had a boyfriend named Chuck, who visited often. I'm told "dada" was the first word I said; the second was "Chuck."

I know I was no more than fourteen months old at the time of this first memory because that's how old I was when Grandma Amy died. It was a car accident that took her. We were all in the car when it happened: Mom, Grandma, and I. It became known in my family as "The Accident," and I'll tell you that story in a bit, but first, where was I? Oh yes, memories. Some linger a lifetime, remaining sharp without apology or reason for hogging up as much memory space as they do. Like my memory of the smell of summer air, breathed deep while pressing my nose against the aluminum screen in our front door. I'm still convinced that heaven will smell like this. Or the one where my four-year-old self sits on the glider in our backyard with my mom as we try to see who can spit cherry pits the farthest.

And what about my childhood address and phone number? Why are they still standing loud and proud on the top shelf of my mind? I've found that to be true with just about everyone.

Other memories gradually shift from technicolor to sepia, fading over time as we strain to recall them. They become a tie-dyed conglomeration of firsthand experience, faded photographs, home movies, and the stories we're told.

The stories held within these pages come from a combination of all the above, and any inconsistencies with the facts are not intentional. There are no tales of sex, drugs, or rock and roll (as evidenced by the first rock and roll album my mom bought me titled, "The Chipmunks Sing the Beatles Hits" by Alvin and the Chipmunks. I'm not kidding).

I've included dialogue in recounting certain events based on my recollections and the stories shared with me. While these conversations capture the essence of what was said, they may not be verbatim. This includes the moment I learned I was adopted. I don't remember that conversation at all, but my mom told me how it went.

Sometimes, however, I can remember conversations word for word. This is most true when the words caused pain. Why are these the words that most often seem to be seared on our memories? I'm not innocent. Some, okay many, of the harsh words I remember today were spoken by yours truly.

Picture my very first memory of this as an example. Molly was seven years older than me and lived down the street from my house. Even before I could walk, she'd come over to my house to play with me, sometimes crawling on the floor with me and sometimes pushing my stroller up and down the sidewalk. When I'm four, she teaches me to square dance to "Turkey in the Straw" as it plays on the record player. I can still see us dosey-doeing around the living room.

By the time I'm six and she's thirteen, she has to wait till I'm home from school before she comes over to play. I try to teach her to play Chutes and Ladders, but no matter how often I try to explain the rules to her, she's unable to grasp the concept. So we turn on the record player for the millionth time and dance to "Turkey in the Straw." I'm tired of the dance and playing the same old things with Molly. I'm also beginning to recognize that I can't talk to her like I talk to my friends at school. Conversations with Molly must be simple, very simple.

When I inform Mom that I don't want to play baby games with Molly anymore, Mom explains that Molly can't do all the same things I do. She says she was just born this way, and she can't help it. She ends with, "You just be nice and keep playing things she can understand."

Molly's mind may not work like mine, but that doesn't mean she doesn't notice that I'm less than excited when she comes over. So, one day she asks me, "Amy, you like me?"

My response? "No." One word that stabs her hopeful question in the heart. And then she starts to cry. I can still see it, hear it, and, worst of all, feel it. Maybe I wouldn't remember that day at all if I'd answered, "Yes, Molly, I like you." But that's not how it happened. I watch Molly walk away from my house while I stand there, surprised and maybe just a little horrified by the power I have at that moment.

When she returns the following day and the day after, and the day after that, she stands at my backyard gate and asks, "Amy, you like me?" And every single time, my response is the same, "No." And every single time, she cries and walks away, returning the following day to repeat it all over again —until she doesn't.

I don't know what happened to Molly. My online search for any record of her has been fruitless. My heart aches to apologize, to wrap my arms around her, and say, "I love you, Molly. I'm so sorry for hurting you." I imagine I'll have to carry the burden of this sad memory until the day I can embrace her in heaven, where I'll find her doing all the things she could never do. And then, just for fun, we'll join hands and dance to "Turkey in the Straw."

In contrast to the memories of all the harsh words I've heard, said, and felt, the memories I have of love and compassion rarely include words at all. Instead, I remember acts: a smile, a loving embrace, the wiping of a tear. No words are necessary for acts of kindness—not a single one. That is the memory of the home I grew up in. Few lovey-dovey words, but the memories of love lived out fill me to overflowing.

As a disclaimer, I understand that not all adoptees have the same loving upbringing and that their adoption experience might be quite different. These adoptees sit heavily on the opinion that adoption is not a good thing, and I completely understand where their opinion is coming from, though I certainly don't agree. The truth is, any time humans are involved, there's a chance they'll mess things up. Not every family is perfect, but that doesn't discredit the value of family. Not every marriage is good, but that doesn't mean marriage itself is flawed. And sadly, not every adopted child finds the love they deserve, but that's no reason to dismiss the amazing, life-changing impact adoption usually has.

In the Beginning

1959 - the year I'm born, and the year I'm adopted by two of the most incredible people on the planet. My dad, Mac, was thirty-four, and my mom, Tena, was forty-six. Between them, they had four adult children from previous marriages, but none together. Mom's twenty-six-year-old daughter, Lou, lived near us, and the day I was born, I instantly became an aunt to her six-year-old son and one-year-old daughter. Lou will have two more children after I'm born, Lori and Earl. These four nephews and nieces have always been like brothers and sisters to me.

Dad was my hero. A little leprechaun of an Irishman with smiling eyes and a Popeye giggle that could charm any savage beast. Everyone loved him, and I never heard a harsh word about another human being coming out of his mouth. He joined the Navy at seventeen during World War II. Over his twenty-year naval career, Dad was on three ships that were sunk from under him, but he rarely talked about those battles. He wasn't one who bragged about anything and would rather talk about things that made us all laugh. Dad retired from the Navy when I was one year old and would work another twenty years at the local water treatment plant.

Mom was raised in an abusive household, hiding butcher knives from her father, who, in his drunken rages, would grab a knife and chase her mother around the house. Mom was feisty, and what she said was law in our family. She had a sixth-grade education and several jobs over her life, including factory worker and house cleaner. Mom loved laughter and dancing, leopard print, and sequins. If it didn't have sequins on it, she sewed them on.

Mom and Dad had always planned on telling me I was adopted. It was never going to be a secret. They had a well-constructed conversation planned for when the time was right. Sometimes, though, perfect timing is out of our control. God's timing, however, is perfect.

I'm three years old when Mom and I attend a birthday party for Timmy, who is also adopted. That evening, while Dad is at work and Mom is tucking me into bed, I ask, "Mama, what's 'dopted'?"

"Hmmm?" is her reply, despite knowing exactly what I just asked.

"Dopted. People at the party said Timmy was a 'dopted. What's that?"

All the plans she and Dad had made about sitting down with me when the time was right evaporated. The time was now, right or wrong, and it would be just Mom and me.

"Well," she said. "Adopted means that Timmy didn't grow in his mommy's tummy. His mommy and daddy chose him, and that's very special."

"Okay."

"And you know what? You're adopted too. You didn't grow in my tummy, but we chose you too! When you were born, we were so excited that you would be our little girl and we love you very much."

"Okay, Mama. I love you, too." And that was that. I was adopted, which meant chosen and special, and I'll share that good news with anyone who'll listen. "Know what? I'm 'dopted."

Just days after learning about my adoption from Mom, I encountered that word in a way that scared me like nothing ever had, giving it a permanent place at the banquet table of my memories.

Picture a perfect spring morning. My three-year-old self is riding a tricycle up and down the sidewalk in front of my house. This particular day, our next-door neighbor, Gerta, who is in her seventies and stands less than five feet tall, comes out her front door and yells at me from the porch, "Why don't you ride your trike in front of a truck, you no-good adopted brat?"

She isn't asking me a question I have to answer. Even at three, I know this. And, there was that word again, *adopted.* I have never been yelled at like this before, and I stop peddling, frozen, in front of her house. She yells again, throwing her arms out toward me as if she's casting a spell and that her waving arms alone will push me out into the street, "Go on with you, you no-good adopted brat!"

There it is again, *adopted.* It doesn't sound like a good word coming from Gerta's mouth. I lean over my handlebars, peddling as fast as I can towards my house with a brand new realization—the witch from Hansel and Gretel lives next door to me.

I run up our porch stairs and into the house, the screen door slamming behind me as my wails break out. Mom can barely decipher the story between my sobs. She sits me down at the kitchen table with a popsicle and tells me, "Stay here and eat your popsicle. I'll be right back," and out the door she goes. Ignoring her instructions, I run to the door with my popsicle and watch her through the screen. I know she's going to Gerta's house. I stand by that door waiting for her with the popsicle dripping down the front of my sundress, hoping Gerta doesn't shove Mom into the magic oven I'm sure she has. Just a couple minutes later, I see Mom coming back towards the house and I run back to the kitchen table. I'm never told, or maybe I just don't remember, what happened between Mom and Gerta that day, but I know that Gerta never yells at me again. In fact, she never speaks to me again for the rest of her life and I avoid her like my life depends on it, always running past her house, never walking. If I'm playing in my yard and my ball goes over the fence into her yard, I ask Dad to go over and get it. If Dad isn't home, the ball stays there until he gets home. I never ask Mom to get it for me, and I'm not sure why. By the time I'm twelve, I'm almost a foot taller than Gerta, but whenever I pass her house, my pace picks up and so does my heart rate. I can't get over the feeling that something evil lives in that house.

But back to my adoption story, which I will hear in dribs and drabs over the course of about six years. Following is the story I'm told as written by Mom, simply and inelegantly, taken from my "An Adopted Child's Memory Book" under the heading "Your Personal History—This is what we did to find *you*."

"*Daddy was stationed in San Diego and we lived in a court of 17 apartments. I managed the apartments. A young couple named Frank and Jean Vazquez came had rented an apartment from us. They had a little boy named Tommy not 2 years old yet. We got to know Jean real well. Her husband was out every night and Jean would sit alone, her and little Tommy. One day she came to use our phone. Said she wanted to talk to her Dr. about adopting out her unborn child. Frank and her were separating and he would be out of the Navy in 3 months and she would get no support from him for either child. She said she couldn't take Tommy and a baby to live at her mother's. It would just be too much. I said, "Oh Jean, we'd love to take the baby." That nite Daddy and I went over and talked to Jean. We all agreed we would adopt the baby when it was born.*

Later that month, Jean and Tommy moved away to live with Jean's brother. That didn't last long. Jean and I kept in touch by mail and we received a letter that Jean and Tommy had gone to her mother's house. I was worried as maybe Jean wouldn't come back to California to have her baby, but her and Tommy came back two months before you were born and took an apartment next door to us. They ate all their meals with us, just slept in their apartment. Grandma and I took Jean and Tommy out to eat to celebrate Jean's twenty-first birthday and we always took them with us to the grocery store and etc. every time we went. We always let Tommy ride the horses outside the stores and always bought him a toy. He liked Grandma, and me, and we loved him.

At last, on a Friday evening, Jean went to the hospital to have you. While Daddy and Grandma kept Tommy, I went to the hospital with Jean and stayed till you were born. Jean was so glad she had a baby girl for us. She named you the name we had chosen, "Amy" after your Grandma Amy and "Robin" after your niece, Robin. Grandma, Tommy and I took Jean and you home to our apartment when you were one and a half days old. The next week, we went to the courthouse and signed legal papers for us to adopt you. Jean and Tommy stayed with us for two weeks till Jean's mother came and picked them up. We paid all hospital and doctor bills as Jean had no money. A month later, I received a phone call from Jean's mother. Jean took real sick and in two days time had died. Seemed like God had planned for us to care for you."

For years, my memory book containing these words has been stored high on a shelf, along with several other photo albums in Mom and Dad's bedroom closet. Not hidden but of little importance to me. I stand on a chair and pull the book down when I'm about nine years old to look through it, but find I have little interest in how old I was when I took my first step or lost my first tooth, and I don't bother reading this long story Mom has recorded there. There's no need. I've heard the story so often I can recite it by heart.

"We always felt so sorry for Jean," Mom would say. "All she had was that little boy. She didn't seem to have any friends. She was so quiet and spoke so little that Tommy hardly spoke at all. Our attorney recommended Daddy and I pose as Jean's aunt and uncle because, at forty-six, I would be considered too old to adopt. So that's what we did. Jean wouldn't hold you or give you a bottle or anything for the two weeks she stayed with us after you were born. I think it must have been easier for her that way. When Jean's mother arrived to pick her and Tommy up, Jean asked if her mom could come in and see you and, of course, we said she could. But when Jean went out to the car and spoke to her mother through the open car window, she looked back at me, waved, and got in the car and drove away. A few months later, we received a telegram telling us that Jean had died."

When I ask Mom what she thinks Jean may have died from, she says, "The telegram didn't say, but I think she must have died of a broken heart."

"Can you do that? Die of a broken heart?" I ask.

"I'm sure you can." She says.

the day my adoption is final

My adoption was final on October 27, 1959, when I was eight months old.

So, that is the story I was told about how I came to be theirs—the end. It's the story I repeat whenever I'm asked about my adoption. It's a beautiful story until you get to the dying part.

Dad never told the dying part. Dad never lied.

"The Accident"

Other than my aforementioned memory of Grandma Amy's lower appendages, the only other memories I have of her come from the stories I'm told, along with a few photos and a couple of black-and-white home movies with no sound.

grandma Amy, mom and me

When I'm fourteen months old, Mom, Grandma, and I are all ready to go shopping for a lampshade when Grandma's brother, Elmer, pulls into the driveway. Grandma tells Mom, "Quick, take off your coat so Elmer doesn't know we're leaving, and we can sit and chat for a while." Grandma loved to talk, she loved to laugh, and she always loved visitors.

Uncle Elmer was an insurance agent who owned his own insurance agency. His office was in the front of his house, which I thought was the neatest thing ever. I imagined my dad never having to leave home to go to work. How great that would be. Uncle Elmer always wore a suit and tie. He was the only one in my family who dressed that way. He and his house smelled like pipe smoke, and when I got older, he always offered me Sen-Sen, a rice-grain-sized piece of potent anise-flavored candy. I hated that little black candy, but I always graciously accepted it, which I felt was the polite thing to do. Smiling, I'd place it on my tongue, then go to another room and spit it out.

But back to May 4th. After an hour-long visit, Uncle Elmer finally leaves, and Mom, Grandma, and I head to the lampshade store. Mom is driving our station wagon, and I'm perched on Grandma's lap in the front seat—no car seat laws in 1960. We wait at a stoplight to cross a four-lane highway with a median until our light turns green, and we enter the intersection. A semi-truck driver named Bert is stopped at the red light for the cross traffic, and he will tell the following story to the police.

As he watches our car enter the intersection, a car speeds past him on his driver's side. It never slows as it slams into the passenger side of our car. He watches in horror as our car flips over twice before landing on its roof, spinning like a top and ejecting the three of us. The collision throws Grandma to the west and Mom to the east, both bodies skidding and tumbling to a stop on either side of the highway. But what he remembers most vividly is seeing my fourteen-month-old body flying through the air and landing directly on top of Mom.

The only sounds Bert hears are my screams as he runs toward Mom and me. Mom and Grandma are silent. He kneels down beside Mom and lifts me off her body as I continue to scream. He tries to clear the gravel that fills Mom's mouth so she can breathe. It's an almost impossible task because her teeth have been driven through both of her lips. Mom doesn't know why she can't open her mouth to form the words she's trying to say, "The baby . . . the baby . . . the baby . . . "

But Burt finally understands and tells her, "The baby is fine, ma'am. It's you we have to worry about."

Thankfully, the accident happened just blocks from the fire department, and it's not long before the paramedics arrive. Grandma is crying out, "Oh, my God! Oh, my God!" A never-ending prayer filled with pain and fear as the paramedics attempt to stabilize her for transport. "Ma'am, can you tell us how much you weigh?" They ask loudly over her cries.

"180," Grandma tells them. Now, Grandma, who hasn't weighed less than 225 pounds for over thirty years, proves that even in our most dire and life-threatening moments, vanity prevails.

Hearing Grandma's weight claim and fearing they'll drop her, Mom tries to yell, "More!" Mom doesn't know that being dropped would be the least of Grandma's problems.

As the rescue vehicles pull away, Bert stays behind to tell the police what he witnessed. He then returns to his truck, pulls it over to the shoulder of the highway, lays his head on his steering wheel, and cries.

Grandma suffers many injuries, including two broken legs, a broken arm, and massive internal injuries. Mom's most severe injuries include five compound fractures of her pelvis and critical spinal injuries. The lady who ran the red light and hit our car is uninjured.

Mom can't see Grandma while the doctors attend to both of them in the emergency room, but she can hear her mother's every groan.

"Ho-hum, ho-hum, ho-hum" are the only words Grandma says. Over and over and over, she says them—and then she stops. Grandma is gone. She was seventy years old.

My only physical injuries appear to be cuts and abrasions. Mom tells me later that the doctors can't believe I'm uninjured, and for that reason, I'll spend seven days in the hospital under observation. My minor physical injuries fade, but the emotional remnants won't become apparent until the next time I ride in a car. If a car approaches from the passenger side where I'm seated, I grab the dash and won't stop screaming. For more than a year after the accident, I will travel lying down in the backseat so I can't see out the windows.

Truck driver Bert stops by the hospital to see Mom the following week and helps her fill in the blanks. He shares with her the story I've written here and explains that he didn't make it to his destination that day. He says he had to go home and hug his wife and daughter and finishes by saying, "It must have been an angel that carried your baby. It was like she was traveling in slow motion right to your body. I've never seen anything like it. It's something I'll never forget."

If only I could have thanked him.

Mom would remain in the hospital, in traction, for over three months. When she is finally discharged, she doesn't know that she'll never completely recover, that her back pain will be a constant reminder of the day her mother died, or that for the rest of her life, she'll have to sit on a donut pillow and keep a little block of wood under her foot whenever she sits at the sewing machine. She doesn't know that she'll always have purple scars on her nose and, every once in a while, a piece of road gravel will pop right out of her skin.

The only thing Mom knows for sure is that she'll always miss Grandma and that she's thankful to be alive to raise the baby that God brought into her life and onto her lap that fateful day in May.

Downtown

Death visits my world regularly after Grandma dies. Many of Mom's relatives are of advanced age, so I hear the words *funeral* and *wake* far more often than I hear *wedding* or *baby shower*. As these people she loves leave us, I take her hand and tell her, "Don't cry, Mama," whenever I see her wiping her tears with the hanky she keeps in the apron she always wears.

I'm six years old when I attend my first wake, but it's not for one of these older relatives. This wake is for Evie, my friend's five-year-old sister, who was hit by a car on her way to kindergarten.

Mom drives us downtown to the funeral home, a red-brick, Victorian-style house with two stories. The wrap-around porch is lined with potted ferns and filled with crying people. As we climb the stairs, I cling to Mom's hand tightly, my fear growing with each step. Despite her gentle explanations, I'm still apprehensive about walking through those doors and facing what lies ahead.

Entering the building, I'm hit with the overpowering fragrance of flowers and sounds of sobbing. I see Evie's mother, father, and sister, Blanca, sitting next to the little white casket where Mom tells me Evie is lying.

I stand a little closer to Mom as we take our place at the back of the line that's inching closer to the casket. Arriving at the front of the line, Mom hugs Evie's mom, and I hug Blanca, who starts to cry, which makes me cry, too. It was only two weeks ago that Blanca and Evie were at my sixth birthday party, and we were all laughing and clapping when Evie put the tail on the donkey's nose during the pin-the-tail-on-the-donkey game. Now we both stand silently, holding hands and looking at Evie, who is wearing a white dress with crystal beads that sparkle in the candlelight and holding Rosary beads in her little hands that lie crossed on her chest. I swear I can see her breathing, and I can't help but feel that the grownups may have gotten it all wrong. It looks to me like she's just sleeping and may wake up any second. Maybe that's why they call it a "wake." Perhaps everyone is standing around just waiting for her to wake up. My spirit lifts at this possibility, but then Mom puts her hand on my shoulder and tells me it's time to go. I give Blanca another hug. It will be the last time I see her. Staying in the house where Evie lived and on the street where she died must have been too painful for her family, so in a week, they're gone.

This experience will forever change how I perceive death; it's no longer something that only happens to old people. It also deepens the sincerity of my bedtime prayers., "If I should die before I wake, I pray the Lord my soul to take." They're not just words. It could happen.

When Mom and I get home from the wake, I put on my pajamas and sit next to her on the couch while we watch Petula Clark sing "Downtown" on the Ed Sullivan Show. To this day, that song will forever transport me back to that day, like a supernatural time machine, and I'm again sitting on the couch with my mom while my six-year-old brain contemplates life and death.

Revisiting these moments from this side of my life makes it clear to me why I feared the death of my parents. It didn't help that Mom was prone to pneumonia. Every winter she'd get it and often ended up in the hospital. She never wanted Dad to bring me to the hospital to see her because she knew she'd cry, and she didn't want to scare me. What she didn't realize was that not seeing her scared me more. I was sure that one day she wouldn't come home. I feared her death throughout my childhood and can't count the number of nights I cried myself to sleep as I imagined that day.

When my daughter recently planned for my granddaughter's first sleepover at someone else's house, she asked me how old I was when I went for my first sleepover —sleeping in a house away from my mom and dad? Never happened. I'd be so excited at the idea, though, packing my bag and imagining the fun to be had, but every single time, I failed. As soon as darkness fell, I'd start crying to go home. I just knew one of my parents would die if I wasn't home to protect them. So the call would go out, "Amy wants to come home." Talking to me didn't help, so Mom or Dad simply said, "We'll be right there."

I never got over this, and eventually, we simply stopped trying. My poor parents never had a single night to themselves.

Sunday School & Jesus Shoes

My journey of faith began with my parents, as many do. Dad grew up in an Irish Catholic family and served as an altar boy at his church. However, a few years later, when that same church refused to baptize his infant son because his first wife wasn't Catholic, he vowed never to return and declared himself finished with organized religion.

Mom came from a long line of Jesus-loving, Bible-believing, gospel-singing Christians. I have tape recordings of family gatherings from the 1950s with the adults singing hymns, in harmony, no less. Grandma Amy's "Ethel Mermanesque" voice overpowers everyone else's when she belts out, "Standing in the Need of Prayer," accompanied by ladies banging on pie tins. Mom loves the old Christian hymns and can't get through a single one without crying.

I'm just two months old when Dad breaks his vow to never step foot in a church again. This comes after Mom informs him they will raise me to know Jesus and that going to the Christian church up the street will be a regular Sunday event for our family. Two years later, on Easter, Dad gets baptized there, and it will be my church home for the first twenty-two years of my life.

The day dad got baptized

I'm taught to pray that familiar bedtime prayer, *"Now I lay me down to sleep. I pray my Lord my soul to keep. If I should die before I wake, I pray the Lord my soul to take."* followed by my request for God to bless a list of people and pets. My memory book says I could recite this prayer by myself at twenty-three months and sing a "Jesus Loves Me" solo three months later.

I attend Sunday School in the basement of our church every Sunday while Mom and Dad meet with the rest of the adults for the sermon upstairs. Mom always ties a few coins into a handkerchief for my Sunday school offering. The knot is always too tight, and every week I struggle to free those coins. One Sunday morning, an older woman sits alone at the end of my row. It's unusual for an adult to be seated in the rows of children, and I can't take my eyes off her. She seems lonely somehow. As the offering basket starts its journey and little hands pass it down each row, I'm concerned that the woman doesn't appear to have any coins in her hand. Maybe she's sad about having nothing to give, I think. So I work twice as hard to get my coins out of my hanky. Stumbling over the kids seated between us, I reach her just as the basket does and hand my coins to her. "For the offering," I say (lest she think of using them to buy a candy bar). I'll never forget her smile.

The best day at Sunday school is the day you get to go to the front of the class during your birthday week to drop your offering into a large wooden cross bank while everyone recites "Many happy returns on the day of thy birth, may sunshine and gladness be given. May God, in His mercy, prepare you on earth for that beautiful birthday in heaven." My bedtime prayer and this birthday prayer confirm my fear that death may be right around the corner.

On Thanksgiving, our house transforms into a bustling family carnival with aunts, uncles, and "cousins by the dozens," as Dad puts it. We've got tables stretching from the dining room into the living room, all overflowing with traditional Thanksgiving culinary delights. We pray before the meal, and after stuffing ourselves, everyone sings Christmas carols as I accompany them on the organ (yes, the organ, just slightly less cool than the accordion), officially welcoming in the Christmas season, my favorite time of the year.

When I'm ten, my namesake niece, Robin and I get baptized on Easter morning. We pinky swear to be perfect for the rest of our lives and never to say naughty words like "shoot" or "darn." File that under "Pinky Swear Fail."

At twelve, I accompany a friend's church group to the Billy Graham Crusade in Chicago. I'm excited to ride the bus into Chicago without my parents like I'm truly grown up. As we enter the McCormick Place Amphitheater, the atmosphere can only be described as electric. I've never seen so many people in one place. Seated near us is a group of "Jesus People," street Christians whom I know nothing about, but they seem so happy, smiling and hugging everyone. They also look like the coolest people I've ever seen.

When the choir begins to sing "Just as I Am," Billy Graham invites everyone to come forward and accept Jesus Christ as Lord and Savior. I know I've already done this when I was baptized, but I can't remain in my seat. My friend and I, and hundreds of others, walk to the stage and invite Jesus into our hearts. I know he's already there because I've heard He never declines a heartfelt invitation, but I figure it won't hurt to invite Him a second time, just to be sure.

Riding the bus home, I decide I'm going to be one of those Jesus People. I'll grow my hair long, wear bell bottoms, and most importantly, save my allowance to buy the same Bible the Jesus people carried with them, the one with "The Way" printed on the cover.

The next day, I write "Jesus" on the rubber toes of my Keds sneakers. My journey as a Jesus Person has begun. As I'm sitting on my porch steps with my Jesus shoes on, a boy walks by and points to my shoes. "Who's Jesús?" he asks, using the Spanish pronunciation.

I freeze. This is my big chance. But all that comes out of my mouth is, "He lives over there," while pointing down the street. He shrugs and walks away. I look down at my Jesus shoes in disgrace. I have failed at my first opportunity to be a Jesus Person. My first opportunity was also my last while wearing my Jesus shoes. No one ever again points to my toes and asks me who Jesus is.

However, that Bible with "The Way" on the cover sets in motion my understanding of the Word of God in a way I can finally understand. In my teenage script, these words are written inside the front cover: "*Lord Jesus, I need You. I open the door of my life and receive You as my Savior and Lord. Thank You for forgiving my sins. Take control of the throne of my life. Make me the person You want me to be.*"

When Worlds Collide

Six weeks after starting the third grade, it's decided that I'll be moved into the fourth grade after my achievement test scores are reviewed. I'll be leaving all my friends and now be a year younger than all the kids in my class, and I'm not sure how I'm feeling about the whole thing as they pull my desk down the hallway. All eyes focus on me as they drag my desk into my new classroom and put it into place. I walk behind it, carrying my coat and wishing I was invisible. It's all quite horrifying for someone who hates attention and just wants to fit in. It's not long before everyone in the class knows I came from the third-grade classroom, and let's just say it doesn't exactly earn me any popularity points. I think it can't possibly get worse. Spoiler alert: I'm wrong.

A few weeks later, I'm walking out of my yard on the way to school when I see the giant white letters spray-painted on the side of our green garage.

HONKY

I'm more alarmed that someone painted on our garage than by the word itself because I don't even know what it means. I imagine a clown with an aruga horn and a honking red nose. Running back into the house, I yell, "Somebody painted our garage!" and Mom and Dad rush out to see.

"What does it mean?" I ask.

"Just kids playing a prank. You go on to school," Dad says, shaking his head.

"What kind of prank is that?" I ask. Again, I'm told to never mind and go on to school.

Standing in the playground before the bell rings, I share the story about the word painted on our garage, and that's when I get my answer. "That's 'cause ya'll white," an older boy shouts as his friends laugh and slap hands. The laughing and slapping hands are worse than the word's meaning, like a celebration of the word that is no longer funny. It now bears sharp edges with pointy corners intended to wound, like every racial epithet since the beginning of time has been meant to do.

Don't get me wrong, it's not that I'm unaware that there are way fewer white faces at my school than there are black and brown ones; it's just that it never seemed to matter. The neighborhood I've lived in since the day I was born has always been racially and culturally diverse, and the friendships were never based on skin color. But now, the word on our garage has called us out because of the color of our skin. Again, feeling like I don't fit in is the worst part for me. It always has been.

Dad has painted over the word by the time I get home from school. The green paint doesn't match exactly, and the blotch will remain to remind me.

A few weeks later, following the first snow of the season, I take my sled to the sledding hill at a nearby park. After several rides down the hill, I see Yolanda, a girl from my class who's been threatening to beat me up after school for weeks. Empty threats so far, but when I see her there with a group of her friends, I stand paralyzed, hoping she won't notice me as I try to devise my exit strategy. But, of course, she does see me and flashes her fist at me again, like she does every day at school.

When she heads toward me with her entourage, I follow my instincts and run in the opposite direction, pulling my sled behind me. Run may be an exaggeration. Did I mention I'm wearing my green puffy coat with matching snow pants that are a size too big and equally oversized black rubber boots over my shoes (because Mom likes outerwear I can grow into)? What I'm wearing only accentuates the reality that I've never been confused with a runner, so I'm easily overtaken. As several hands pull the sled from my grip, I lose my balance and fall on my back. I throw my arms over my face to protect it from the snow being kicked at me as they hurl a barrage of insults, many of which start with the word *white*. My white butt (though "butt" is not exactly the word they use) features prominently in the diatribe. I don't understand why my butt, which is indeed white, is such an object of ridicule. I've heard most of their insults before, but some are wrapped in cuss words that are new to me. I'm eight years old and lay there like a green slug, wondering if I'll live to be nine. Even after they stop their snow assault, my arms remain over my face because I know it will be worse if they see me crying. Eventually tiring of the game, they walk away laughing—with my sled. And as a parting gift, they yell, "Your mama's a hoe!" The kids who have stood idly by watching the show are laughing, too. I hate the laughing. I've never felt so alone.

Finally, I peek out from under my arms and, seeing I'm alone, get up and walk as fast as I can towards home. Looking over my shoulder to make sure no one is following me, I slow to a trudge and think about those last words, "Your mama's a hoe," while I try to extract a meaning from that particular garden implement that's obviously meant as an insult. I've got nothing.

My thoughts turn to my sled, or more accurately, my missing sled, and how I'm going to explain that fact to my mom. I contemplate my options. Lie and tell her I lost it. She'll never believe that, and I can't ever remember lying to my parents. If I tell her the truth, she'll either make me go back and get it or go there herself. I don't know which would be worse. Maybe if I say nothing, she won't notice and eventually think someone stole it off our porch. Still lying by omission, but it feels less wrong somehow, so I settle there.

The sun is low on the horizon as I approach my house and see the porch and kitchen lights are on. I sneak up the porch steps and take off my boots, hoping Mom won't notice my sled-less appearing. Then I enter the house like nothing has happened and see Mom peeling potatoes at the sink.

"Hi, Mom!" I say in my most chipper voice as I shed my snow gear. "Need some help?" She stops what she's doing and looks at me. No wonder. I've never offered to help prepare supper before.

I quickly change the subject. "Mom, what's a hoe?"

"What do you mean?" She's back to peeling. "You know what a hoe is."

"Some kids at the park called you hoe, and that doesn't make sense." I desperately want to pull the words back into my mouth the minute they're out there hanging in the air. Why did I tell her they called *her* a name, something that may tip her off to my less-than-normal sledding experience?

That look comes over Mom's face again. It's the same look she had when she saw the word painted on our garage. "I don't think that's what they meant."

"So what did they mean?"

"How about you look it up in the dictionary?"

I don't know why she won't just tell me, but I get the dictionary from the desk, sit down at the table, and spell out loud, "H O . . . "

"No, the word they were saying starts with a W. w-h-o-r-"

"Whore?" I ask when I see the word. I don't wait for confirmation as I continue to read, "a person who engages . . ." I stop. "Oh." It's all I can say as the heat of embarrassment floods over me at the horror of what I'm reading. Now I understand why she told me to look it up. We don't discuss things of this nature in my home. In fact, a year ago, when kids were talking about where babies come from, I proudly proclaimed, "I'm adopted. My parents don't do stuff like that."

Mom continues putting supper together, unfazed, as if that word meant the Queen of England instead of—well, you know. I don't want to talk about this, and I now feel like I may throw up.

"Just ignore people when they say things like that did you put your sled away?" She says it just like that without a period or a breath between sentences. I'd already forgotten about the sled, but after her question, The grandfather clock seems louder than usual, *tick-tock-tick-tock-tick-tock*. How do I get out of this? I can't. She looks up when I don't answer, "Well?"

"No. No, I didn't,"

"Go back out and put it in the garage. We don't want it to go missing."

I don't move, and the silence sucks the air out of the room as I try to figure out how I can spin this story without boldface lying to her. There is no way out.

"They took it," I say under my breath. Maybe she won't hear and forget the question. I know better.

"Who took it?" she asks.

"Some kids at the park." I don't tell her it's the same kids who called her that name.

Untying her apron, she heads to the closet, "Get your coat on. We're going to get it."

Worse than I expected. We're both going. "Aw, Mom, just let 'em have it. I don't need a sled. I don't really like sledding that much, anyway." And that part is true. I may never go back.

"Don't be ridiculous. We worked hard for the money it took to buy that sled, and stealing is wrong. Now get your coat on, and let's go." She's already got her purse, has put on her boots, and is out the door.

We get in the car. Mom's on a sled recovery mission while, over the four-block route, I try to devise a plan to keep her from being killed. How can I make her understand the danger she's in? Arriving at the park, she gets out of the car, and I make no move to do the same. She walks around to the passenger side and opens my door.

"Come on." It's her stern voice, which means I have no recourse.

Groaning, I get out of the car and begin our trek to the sledding hill. "Do you see the kids who took your sled?" she asks, scanning the hill that now glows under the park lights and where a couple of dozen kids are sledding.

What if I just tell her I don't? *Liar, liar, pants on fire,* the voice in my head answers, and like it has a life of its own, my arm raises, and my mitten-covered hand points at the girls with my sled. "That's them." *As my brain whispers, "You better hope they don't see you turning them in."*

Mom starts towards my sled. "Come on."

"I don't want to. Please, Mom, they're going to kill you." I'm whining now.

Shaking her head in frustration, she says, "They're not going to kill me." She turns, and I watch as she walks away, resembling a five-foot two-inch Q-tip, her white bouffant hair shellacked and unmoving in the frigid breeze. Then she's approaching my sled bearers like a stormtrooper, and less than a minute later, she's walking back towards me, pulling my sled behind her while Yolanda raises her fist at me—again. I dread what tomorrow holds, and all I can hope is I'll die in my sleep.

We return home. "Now put the sled in the garage and come in and set the table," Mom says as if that's it. Life has returned to normal—just another day. But it doesn't feel like just another day. My thoughts swirl in my head and keep my heart beating like a steel drum in my chest as I imagine what the future holds.

When tomorrow comes, nothing changes. No worse, no better. Yolanda flashes her fist at me whenever the teacher's back is turned—a shove here and an "accidental" elbow jab there. I stop drinking water at school so I won't have to go to the girls' restroom because it feels like a dangerous place with no adult eyes present. Recess and gym class are my two greatest fears, especially the team-picking ordeal. Being picked last is like a cruel cosmic joke, and to this day, I'd love to meet the sadistic genius who invented dodgeball. Nothing says "fun" like being a human target in your own personal game of survival.

Why don't I tell my teacher or my parents about the bullying? The answer is simple. Yolanda has promised that my parents will be killed and my house burned down if I ever tell anyone, and right or wrong, I believe her. It's psychological warfare in its most basic form.

As crime increases and sirens become a regular sound in our neighborhood, Dad puts padlocks on our chain-link gates. It's hardly a stealth security measure since our fence is only four feet tall, but it marks the day I'm no longer allowed outside after dark. One night, we hear gunshots followed by sirens, and the police car lights reflect on our wall through the crack in the drawn living room drapes. We move to the den in the back of the house to be safe. The next day, while walking up my driveway after school, I hear a deafening popping noise and feel the air move as what I assume is a bullet passes my ear. Was I just shot at, or was I just in the wrong place at the wrong time? It doesn't matter. That the wrong place and time is my driveway at 3:30 in the afternoon means my neighborhood is no longer safe in the daytime either. When I ask Mom why we can't move away from this neighborhood like so many of my friends have, she tells me, "This has been my family home for many years. Everything will be fine." Right.

When Yolanda starts calling me at home with threats of my impending doom, I stop eating, and Mom figures out something is wrong ("What do you mean, you don't want a Twinkie?"). I finally break, spilling my guts and through sobs, tell her everything that's been happening over the year at school and all about Yolanda, the girl who hates me. I tell her she's the one who took my sled. I assure her that outside of the threats, name-calling, and some shoves, they've never hurt me physically and add that I'm sure they won't. That last part is a lie, as I'm not sure of that at all, but I am sure that I don't need Mom to show up at my school to take matters into her own hands. When I tell her about the threat to her and Dad's lives and our house, if she tells anyone, she laughs. Clearly, she doesn't understand the danger we are all in and does the exact opposite of what I've asked her to do. She calls the principal, who assures her that the situation will be monitored and that I should let the teacher know if there's ever a problem—as if that's going to happen.

Every Christmas, my school organizes a drive to collect gifts for families in need. Mom is the president of the PTA throughout my grade school years, and every Christmas, she dresses up as Mrs. Claus and sometimes even Santa himself to bring candy canes to all the kids at school and to deliver those collected Christmas gifts. Dad and I pitch in to help with the gifts. My favorite part is helping hand them out; the wrapping, not so much.

When we knock on the door of the first house this Christmas, a mom opens the door with the three youngest children standing beside her. The little ones are clearly excited to see Santa and Mrs. Claus. Then, the four older children come into the room. That's when Yolanda's and my eyes meet, and my heart jumps into my throat. Mom hands me a gift and tells me it's for Yolanda, so I walk over and offer it to her. Her hands, which are usually clenched into fists, reach out to accept the gift. Though smiling at her is difficult, I make the effort and believe she does too. No words are spoken. When Mom and I get back in the car, I tell Mom that was the girl I had told her about. The one making the calls. The one who took my sled. The one who hates me. I leave out the part about Yolanda calling her a "hoe."

"I know who she is," Mom says, "And she doesn't hate you." I don't believe her, but I can tell by her tone that this is the end of the conversation.

Over time, the bullying eases up. It never goes away completely, but I'm 95 percent sure no one is going to kill my parents or burn down my house, and 85 percent sure those fists that are flashed at me aren't actually going to strike me. Gym class, however, will forever remain my nightmare.

Riots and chaos seem to be a constant in our community and schools throughout my school years. By the time I'm a junior, just three months past my sixteenth birthday, I've racked up enough credits to graduate, two full years ahead of schedule, thanks to essentially skipping the third grade. And that's where my school story ends. My primary goal of escaping school is achieved. College never crosses my mind; I only want to get married and have babies.

My entire childhood experience taught me that anyone can be a target of prejudice and bullying because evil has no color or gender. No one is immune. Bullies prey on others to elevate themselves. Some follow the leader of the pack, not sure why the target is the target, but vowing allegiance to the leader out of pride, fear, or ignorance, and so it spreads like the disease it is. To this day, I am hyperaware of anyone in a crowd who may feel singled out. The feeling is so strong it even overpowers the introvert in me as I try to make that person feel welcome or, at least, not so alone.

I was blessed to grow up in a home where my parents taught by example, showing love and forgiveness at all times, even after Mom was mugged on their back porch when she was seventy-four. The thief grabbed her purse and dragged her down the stairs. Maybe if she'd let go of her purse, she could have avoided the dragging part, but she'd "worked hard for that money," you know. She ended up scraped and bruised, but the only thing truly broken was her vow never to leave that house. They finally move away from the home Mom had loved for over fifty years, leaving a little piece of her heart behind.

The Girl in the Photo

When I'm eleven, one of the many presents under the Christmas tree is more than just a gift. It's a shift in the alignment of the planets, all wrapped up with a bow. I know before I open it, it's different from any other Christmas present I've ever received because it has an envelope attached to it instead of a gift tag. My name is written on the front of the envelope, and inside is a Christmas card bearing Mom's handwriting. "*We think it's time for you to have these. All our love, Mom and Dad.*"

Inside the box is a framed 8 x 10 black-and-white, slightly blurry photo of a woman. I see myself in her face, and I know instantly that this is my birth mother, Jean.

"Is this Jean?" I ask, though I already know.

"It is." I can see they are waiting for my reaction, and it feels like time has stopped.

This is the first time I've ever seen the face that goes along with my story, a face that looks back at me like I'm looking in a mirror. It's the first face I've ever seen that truly resembles my own. Along with the framed photo are four other black and white snapshots that I pick up one by one and slowly examine. One of Jean sitting on the bumper of a 1950s-era car, and holding a diaper-clad infant who looks to be about nine months old.

"Is this Tommy?" I ask.

"Yes, that's your brother, Tommy. That's him in the other two photos, too," says Mom.

Another photo shows Jean smiling sweetly, sitting on the ground under a tree with Tommy sitting slightly behind her, playing in the dirt. The third, more somber, out-of-focus photo is of Jean wearing an unbuttoned coat and sitting on a cement stoop. She's not smiling, and her head is downcast, apparently unaware that the photo is being taken. Tommy is sitting on the step below her.

"You're in that photo," Mom says as I study it.

"I am? Where?" I don't see a baby.

"That's when she was pregnant with you." And there I am — a blurry bulge peeking out from under her coat.

The last picture is a small class photo that matches the enlarged framed photo. The small photo bears the date 1955-1956 on the bottom front and is inscribed on the back with "To Sally, Love Jean" in what I assume is Jean's handwriting, which also looks so much like my own. I run my finger over the handwriting.

I examine each photo again, examining every detail, from Jean's shoes to her earrings. Mom and Dad watch patiently until it feels as if I've stared at these photos for an awkwardly long time. “Wow. I look like her, don’t I? Where’d you get these?”

Mom answers, “You do look like her. She gave us those photos and asked us to give them to you someday.” I look up to see Mom dabbing her eyes with a hanky.

Suddenly, I feel as though I’ve hurt her. Why did I show so much interest in the woman in these photos? Like a movie in Fast Forward, I quickly put the photos back in the box, put the lid on, and set it aside. Then, trying very hard to sound casual, I say, “It’s nice to put a face with the story. Thank you so much.” I cross the room and give each of them a hug and a kiss on the cheek. Let Christmas continue, and it does, but that box of photos has changed everything.

I’ve lived eleven years without an inkling of what Jean or Tommy look like and I’ve never felt I’d been missing anything at all in that ignorance. Now, however, I see her face every day, all framed up and looking back at me from my dresser, and for the first time, I feel a connection with her. She becomes more than just a story as she looks back at me from that frame, a daily reminder of who I came from. She is the beginning of me, and that photo becomes the seed from which all my questions will bloom. I hold the photos she once held in her hand, photos she wanted me to have, realizing that she not only cared enough to give me life and give me to parents who would love me, but also wanted me to know she and my brother existed. It feels like a message of love from the grave.

As the years pass, Jean's photo remains on my dresser as my list of questions grows. Where is she buried? Does Tommy put flowers on her grave? Where did he go when she died? Is he living with our father? Where is he today? Does Tommy even know I exist and if so, does he ever think about me?

I also start thinking more and more about that dying from a broken heart thing. What did that really mean? Did she commit suicide because she gave me away? That question holds too much responsibility, so I quickly push it aside. The questions are not much more than the ponderings of an idle mind until they begin to take on a life of their own.

When Fairy Tales Short Circuit

At seventeen, I marry the boy who has been my best friend from the time I was twelve years old. Having a child is all I've ever wanted, and that will not happen without getting married, as far as I'm concerned. Giving birth to my daughters is more than the typical birth experience for me. For the first time ever, someone in my life shares my DNA, and when I look into the eyes of these little humans, I see a little piece of me. I'm also curious about their genealogy. Who else am I seeing glimpses of? A grandmother's nose? A grandfather's

ears? How many generations had to come together at just the right time and place for these little ones to exist? Does anyone else think about stuff like this? Should it matter that the pieces missing from my story are also missing from theirs? I don't know if it should, but it does.

While discussing one of the many adoption questions that randomly pop into my head with my husband, he asks me, "How do you know your birth mother is dead?" The question, asked so casually, is like a glass of cold water to my face. I've never once considered the possibility that Jean could be alive.

"What do you mean? Of course, she's dead. Mom and Dad got the telegram."

"I know, but where's the telegram? Have you ever seen it?"

My brain short circuits at the thought of it. Other than what I've been told, what proof do I have? Why didn't Mom keep that historical telegram? I look through my memory book again and see the lock of hair from my first haircut and a tiny first bandaid. There is no telegram. All the questions that have lived comfortably and pretty politely in my brain now move out of the way so this one question can spin like a ninja warrior in my head.

Is Jean still out there somewhere? And if so, is she alive and living the dream, or alive and living in a mental hospital convinced she's the queen of a faraway land populated by talking squirrels? Despite the crazy scenarios, the question remains: Could Jean be alive? Every once in a while, the question creeps into my mind like an unwelcome visitor, but I quickly push it aside. Raising my daughters is my top priority, and I don't have the time to dwell on speculations about my birth mother.

Master Class in Humility

My marriage comes to an end after five years when my daughters are two and four. The divorce is amicable, and we explain it away as "We were too young. We grew apart. Blahdy blahdy blah." Easy words for something that's not.

The pastor from our church shows up at my door when he hears the news of our impending divorce. I'm expecting kind words of encouragement and hope, but when I turn down his offer of counseling, he informs me that if I go forward with this divorce, I'll prove I have been living a lie. He walks out my door, leaving behind a distinct feeling that I will no longer be welcome at the only church I've ever known. And with that, a little piece of me dies.

The divorce has put me in a tough spot financially. Even though we separated on good terms, the child support I'm getting is barely enough. I'm facing the reality of needing a job or applying for public assistance. The thought of not being home to raise my daughters, which is all I've ever wanted, is really hard to accept. So here I am at the welfare office, clutching my application with my daughters beside me, surrounded by a room full of people also seeking help. At that moment, it hits me hard that I'm not so different from anyone else here. I believed "God helps those who help themselves" was a fundamental biblical truth. One that justified my self-reliance and, if I'm honest, also fed my pride. Now, though, my situation feels like a direct challenge to everything I once believed about strength, independence, and need, leaving my pride exposed and vulnerable.

Years later, I'll learn that "God helps those who help themselves" isn't a Bible verse at all. I'll discover that the Bible offers a different message about God helping those who are vulnerable and in need, regardless of their ability to help themselves. But for now, I'm sitting in the front row of a crash course on humility, unaware that this will be just the first of many lessons to come.

I wear my oldest clothes when I go grocery shopping, and as we reach the checkout, I tell my girls to "look sad," hoping that our pitiful appearance will win sympathy from the cashier instead of judgment. My face flushes with embarrassment as I pull out the food stamps from my purse. Is my fear of judgment because I had judged others? It's a hard truth to face and is both humbling and life-changing. I often thought, "There, but for the grace of God go I," but maybe this is God's grace in action, teaching me how to walk in someone else's shoes by putting them on my feet.

After six months of public assistance, I give up my cherished role as a stay-at-home mom to take a federal job as an administrative assistant while my parents look after my daughters.

When I receive my first check, my heart sinks. How is it possible to end up with less money working for the government than I was receiving from the government to stay home and be a mom to my daughters? I'm miserable being away from my little girls and spend every break and lunchtime crying in the restroom.

Four months later, I marry for the second time. Mark, who is twenty-two years older than me, is a kind and gentle man who is good to me and, most importantly, to my girls. It also means I can return to my stay-at-home mom status.

Kitchen Sink Moments

To say I love my parents is an understatement, and the last thing I want to do is hurt them. It's not like I need another mother, but the questions in my head won't stop. I tell myself that if I prove that Jean really did die, I'll be able to let all my questions die right along with her. I have no idea what I'll do if I find out she didn't. Either way, I have to know, so I call the San Diego County Recorders Office and ask how I would go about getting a copy of her death certificate. I follow the instructions by sending a written request and a $5.00 check to cover the processing fee. A few weeks later, I receive an envelope bearing the governmental return address. Inside the envelope is a single sheet of paper stating, "The information you requested is not on file at our office."

I'm neither surprised nor disappointed. I knew it was a long shot since I'm not sure where Jean was living at the time of her supposed death, so this proves nothing. My only question now is, When Jean got into her mother's car and rode away twenty-five years ago, where did she go, and how can I find out without asking Mom and Dad? I can't.

So many of my childhood memories took place in our kitchen. My very first memory of Grandma's legs takes place there, as well as the moment I heard Mom's anguished cry after answering the phone and hearing that JFK had been shot. I was four and had never heard Mom make a sound like that, so I ran to the foot of our stairs and sat there till her crying stopped.

Our most epic and memorable conversations always happened in the kitchen, with Mom at the kitchen sink and Dad at the table, where he'd be sipping coffee and wrestling with a crossword puzzle. So, it's no surprise when that's exactly the scene I stumble into, Mom mid-scrub and Dad mid-argument with 9 Across.

"So I've been thinking . . . I'd like to try to find my brother Tommy. Do you know where Jean was from? Maybe where her mother lived when she went to live with her?"

And, just like that, I've released the Kracken. The silence is deafening.

I look from Mom to Dad and back to Mom, who continues scrubbing.

And then, Dad just casually drops it, "I think she was from Globe, Arizona, wasn't she?" My head whips over to look at Dad, who is now sitting back in his chair and looking at Mom. I turn my gaze to Mom, the verifier of all things, and that's when I see it, the truth—without a single word being spoken. She looks at Dad, and if looks could kill, Dad would be lying in a pool of coffee on top of his crossword puzzle.

It's like time is moving in slow motion, one of those epic scenes where the hero realizes the truth. Except in this case, the hero is me, and the truth is that there was never a telegram announcing Jean's death. Dad seems completely oblivious to Mom's death-ray glare or pretends to be. Then Mom, with her back to me and still scrubbing away, says, "If you find your brother, you'll probably find your mother." There it is, the mic-drop moment of truth, covered in dish soap.

Without skipping a beat, I say, "I know," as if she'd just told me where to find the peanut butter. I'm not even the tiniest bit angry or disappointed about discovering that my entire life was based on a well-crafted lie. Calling it a lie actually feels like the wrong word. I instinctively know why this story was created. It was to protect them from losing me —a way to keep me from looking for my birth mother. And now, as the fairy tale crumbles, I'm left with the reality that it was just an elaborate plot twist.

I will later find out that I was only partially correct in that assessment. That fairy tale? All Mom's idea. She says she told Jean, "We're going to tell her you died, so don't ever think about coming to find her." And just like that, Mom had herself a foolproof plan to keep Jean from showing up on their doorstep or, worse, taking me back.

Mom and Dad had always told me they wanted me no matter who I turned out to be. It didn't matter to them if I was a boy or girl, healthy or sick. When I was born, they would love and care for me no matter what. So how could I be mad about the story Mom cooked up to make sure they'd never lose me?

Years later, Dad confesses that he was against the "Jean died" story from the very beginning but went along with it because, let's be honest, Mom was the boss. She may have been small in stature, but Mom was strong-willed, and, honestly, she ruled the roost. All her life, she called it as she saw it, no holds barred and often without a filter. If Mom felt something was for the best, it was, end of conversation. There was no use arguing with her, and I should add that although I don't share her DNA, she mentored me well in the no-nonsense department.

The reality was that my strong-willed little mom had been plenty scared. She knew there was a waiting period, and Jean had several months to change her mind and take me back. She also knew that Jean might have created a situation at any time since she knew who they were and would easily be able to find them, and me if she really wanted to. Open adoption was practically unheard of. Secrecy and sealed records were the name of the game, and no matter what the law said, Mom was terrified that Jean might show up and whisk me away. What she didn't know was that I had been afraid of the very same thing.

The entire kitchen sink exchange takes less than a minute or two, and I now know there is a very real possibility that Jean is alive and out there somewhere.

Mom continues with her dishwashing, scrubbing like she's trying to wash away all that just happened, while Dad helps me find Globe, Arizona in the book of US driving maps I retrieve from the den.

What If's

Once I decide I'll try to find Jean and Tommy, I join an adoption support group made up almost entirely of adoptees who are searching for their biological families, but birth parents and adoptive parents are also members. The meetings are held in the basement of a church and the room is filled with adults who are all on their own journeys with a wide variety of stories to tell. It's the first time I've been around anyone with the same questions I have, and I feel like these are my people, around whom I can be open and honest with no fear of offending or hurting anyone. We share a common bond, and I feel validated by these complete strangers who put exactly what I've felt my entire life into words.

I can easily identify the adoptees in the group who enter their first meeting and sit at the back of the room in wide-eyed silence as I did at my first meeting. Birth parents are more vocal even at their first meeting, and adoptive parents sit with their adoptees as a sign of unity and support. I never invite Mom and Dad to join me because I want the freedom to ask questions without worrying about hurting their feelings. It never enters my mind that I would later come to regret that decision and envision myself sitting in that meeting next to the most incredible parents I could have ever hoped for. I didn't know then that the words "I wish I would have" would hurt so much.

Many of the adoptees share stories of lives ruled by rejection complexes, just like mine. Why is this such a common trait among us? No matter how much we are loved and wanted by our adoptive families, our fear of rejection holds us hostage. Of all the people in the world, you would think those who felt "chosen" would feel less rejected than anyone, but that doesn't seem to be the case. Being rejected by the first person in your life, the person who the world says should love you unconditionally, well, there's just something about it that leaves a mark, no matter how happy you are with your life.

Gradually, the silent adoptees open up, and the stories about their searches mesmerize me. I hear stories about reunions, both good and bad, and more than a few dead-end frustrations. All the adoptees in the room are searching for birth mothers, though it's perfectly feasible for someone to be looking for a birth father, I suppose. I've never given much thought to my birth father. Why is that? Would I have looked for him if Jean had actually died? Or would he have simply been a byproduct of finding Tommy? I don't know. A part of me may bear a grudge against him for the whole situation. I mean, abandoning his pregnant wife and two-year-old son, leaving her no other option than to place her unborn child for adoption? That doesn't exactly make him the father of the year in my book.

I take a lot of notes at these meetings, including some tips for what to do and what not to do when you're searching for your birth mother.

1—Don't "out" your birth mother. When you talk to people who may have information about your birth mother, be discreet. Keep confidential what is potentially "her secret" of your existence. —Okay. I'll craft my own story—basically, tell a few lies. When I head to Arizona with my photos of Jean and start asking around if anyone knows her, I won't mention that she's my birth mother. Instead, I'll spin a tale that Jean was a school friend of my late mother. I'll say my dearly departed mom often talked about her best friend, Jean, and since I'm passing through the town where they grew up, I thought I'd try to find her because Mom would have liked that. Lies stacked on top of lies. What could possibly go wrong?

2—As excited as you are to meet your birth mother, your birth mother may not be that excited to meet you. In fact, she may be downright angry that you found her. —People share stories with precisely that scenario at these meetings. It doesn't take more than one horror story for my excitement to drown in a sea of doubt and fear. *What am I thinking? She's already rejected me once, but twice? I might never recover.*

3—When you're ready to make that fateful call to someone who may be "the one," be prepared. If you're female, you may recognize your own voice when she answers, but don't let that throw you off. When she answers the phone, say the following in this order:

—"*This is a really important call, so can you take down my number in case we get disconnected?*" Why? Because your birth mother's knee-jerk reaction upon hearing who you claim to be might be to hang up the phone, resulting in your feeling rejected and not likely ever to call back, and when she calms down, she will not know how to reach you. — Great advice in a world before caller ID.

—"*Does <insert your birthdate here> mean anything to you?*" This is a pretty strong hint. But whether she says it does or it doesn't, just keep going with the rest of the details. If she hangs up, don't call back, at least not immediately. — and don't kill yourself. (I add that one.)

Of all the aspects of my search, the first contact call is the most intimidating for me, a person with a well-developed rejection complex. Getting someone to take down my phone number before I start a conversation? You might as well ask me to quote Shakespeare with a mouth full of razor blades. I mean, honestly, who's going to answer a phone and be okay with taking down the phone number of a perfect stranger who they probably feel is just trying to sell them something? How am I ever going to be able to do this?

Members of the support group also help each other with their searches. I'm asked to help a man who is just a few years younger than me, who is attending college in another state and was born in a hospital near me. We eventually find his birth mother, but when he finally makes contact, she informs him that his existence is a product of rape and she wants nothing to do with him. I feel his pain as if it's my own. Could this be how my search will end? Rejection. Yes, with every story I hear, Pandora's box of possibilities overflows. This is my new reality.

Feeling well informed, though not very confident after the adoption support group meetings, I finally plan our trip to Arizona. Mom and Dad will watch the girls, and Mark and I will fly to Arizona and stay with his sister, who, coincidently, lives less than a hundred miles from Globe. As the date of the trip approaches, my fears overwhelm me. What am I thinking? Am I just going to show up in Globe and ask around? What information do I have, really? Her first name, married name, a few old photos, and the name of a town she may have lived in. Should I wait till I have more information? But how do I get more information with so little information?

The chatter in my mind that once taunted me with questions about where I came from and who I really am now become voices of doom and gloom. *Your life is good. Do you really want to take this chance? What if Jean doesn't want to be found and gets angry? What if she and her family come with a truckload of misery? Are you even considering how these people may impact your daughters and your parents? This is just plain selfish. You have parents and a family who've done nothing but love you. They've always been there for you, and now you're going to put them all at risk for what may end up being crazy town. What's the matter with you? She didn't want you in the first place, so what makes you think she'll want you now? And after it's all said and done, you may be wasting your time. She might not even be alive.*

The happily-ever-after reunion story I've imagined for myself turns into the *Psycho* movie with a little less blood — mostly. The scenarios I imagine are a bottomless bucket of ugly that are beyond terrifying, amplified by my overactive imagination, and all playing out in vivid HD before HD is even a thing. I'm nothing if I'm not creative.

The thought of finding my birth mother, that was once drenched in promise, is now bleeding to death. When I add that my desire to know is based more on curiosity than really wanting a relationship, it's almost enough to make me trash the whole idea, but I don't. Even if there's a troll under the bridge, I'll cross the bridge anyway. And if it all leads to dead ends, further rejection, or whatever other horror may lie waiting, at least my brain will stop itching from the questions crawling around in there.

The decision is made despite the protestations of those nagging voices. Still, the scariest question of all remains, tugging at my heart. *Am I hurting the two people I love more than anything in the world*? My parents don't deserve to feel abandoned by me. Do they—can they—will they understand why I need to have my questions answered? How are they really feeling about this? Great questions, but I never ask them. No, instead of asking them how they feel about it, I tell them why I'm doing it. I do it as casually as possible like it's no big deal.

"I really just want to find Jean to get my questions answered, you know? Especially the medical ones," I explain. "I'm not replacing you. I could never replace you. You'll always be my mom and dad, and I love you. You know how you can love more than one child? It's like that," I tell them, "You can love more than two parents."

As the words vomit out of my mouth, I instantly regret saying the stupidest thing I could have said. No love can compare to the love I have for them. Jean carried me, gave birth to me, and loved me enough to let me go, for which I am eternally grateful. But when it comes to raising me and being a parent, she had no part in that. She wasn't there loving me unconditionally for the last twenty-five years. My mom and dad have been. They've always been there for me. If only those were the words I'd said.

Why are there so many "If I only had's" in life? If I only had taken the time to sit down with them and talk about their feelings, but it just wasn't something my family did. We weren't mushy. Not that mushy is bad. In fact, it would have been nice if we had been a little more mushy, but we weren't. We knew we loved each other, but we didn't sit around talking about it. We didn't talk about our feelings at all, for that matter. If they were still alive today, I would ask them how they felt about me finding my birth mother, and I would probably have just the right words to say. Little consolation in having the right words to say when the ears I want to speak them into are no longer here.

The week before I leave for Arizona is Mom's seventy-second birthday. We've always exchanged funny birthday cards because, like I said, we've never been sentimental about much, but this birthday is different. We may not be good about vocalizing our deepest feelings, but I'm leaving in a week on a "Where's Waldo" search for the woman who gave birth to me, and I still feel guilty about searching for a "mother" when I already have all the mother I could ever want. I want more than anything for her to know that.

She knows this birthday card is different when she opens it. There's no knock-knock joke or cartoon of a dancing chicken. The image on the front is beautiful, and the words written inside are in script:

"A mother is someone who dreams great dreams for you,
yet accepts the dreams that you decide to follow,
and always loves you just the way you are.
Thanks for being you and for encouraging me to be me."

Mom grabs her hanky when she reads it, just like I knew she would. This search I'm about to embark on now has my guilt standing at full attention and saluting. It feels like the saddest birthday party ever, and my bite of her birthday cake can barely make it past the lump in my throat as I struggle to hold back the tears.

Activate the Launch Sequence

This will be my second trip to Arizona. I'm told I passed through the state when I was six, and Mom, Dad, and I took our annual two-week car trip around the country to visit friends and family. All the states blend together when you're six years old and sitting in the backseat of a car. I have one photo of me sitting on the edge of a motel pool wearing a bathing cap and a striped bathing suit. The back of the photo is inscribed, "Yuma, Arizona," in Mom's familiar script. That photo is all I remember of Arizona.

Two days before we leave, I dye my bleached blonde hair back to its natural dark brown—the same color as Jean's hair in the photos I have. If I find her, I want to look like my "natural" self to match her "natural" self. I'm now as ready as I'll ever be.

October 2, 1984, is the day we leave for Arizona, and will be remembered as one of the saddest days of my life. My heart is in my throat as I hug my dad that rainy day when he drops Mark and me off at the airport. Walking towards the gate, I look back and see my little daddy standing there waving, wearing his ever-present USS Yorktown baseball cap perched a little crooked on his head and his grey polyester pants hanging just a little too long over his velcro tennis shoes. I wave and smile, but the smile is a lie, and I can't hold back the tears as I turn away. I cry all the way to the gate. I cry all the way to Phoenix with my head pressed up against the airplane window, hoping no one will notice my tears. I can't help but feel I'm betraying the parents who have loved me unconditionally since the day I was born. Did Daddy's heart hurt as much as mine when we waved goodbye? Even as I write this, almost forty years later, the memory of Daddy standing there looking so small as I walk away from him brings tears to my eyes. If I get a role in a movie and have to manufacture tears, this is the image that will make that happen.

As the plane heads towards Phoenix, the urge to pray comes over me. Praying is not something I've done much of unless it's an emergency, like some kind of SOS to God. When my three-year-old was choking on a piece of hard candy and turning blue, for example, I raced toward her, screaming, "Please, God, help her!" My perfect execution of the Heimlich Maneuver, something I'd never even heard of, was obviously an answer to that prayer. Those SOS prayers of desperation are instinctual, like gasping for air after you've been underwater too long and your lungs feel like they're exploding. Those are the prayers I'm good at.

But sitting here on the plane doesn't feel like an SOS prayer; it just feels like I have to talk to God. I've always felt praying is best done by people who are fluent in Bible-is, who can speak to God, who is far too holy to be approached by someone like me. When I try to pray with perfect words, I fail every time. But right now, I pray like I'm talking to the Father God, speaking quietly and drowned out by engine noise, "Dear God, it's me, Amy. Please keep my mom and dad safe while I'm in Arizona. If they die while I'm gone, I won't be able to live with myself if going off to find Jean is the last thing they feel.—*Yes, their possible deaths are still at the forefront of my nightmares.* Please bring me back home to them so they'll know that I could never replace them and that they will always be my one and only mom and dad. Please, oh please, keep them and my girls safe while I'm away. Thank You. Amen." I feel better, though a part of me wonders if God even remembers who I am.

A Photo, a Name, and a Prayer

When we arrive at my sister-in-law's house, we spend the afternoon sharing stories with her, along with the details of my upcoming search for answers. The following morning, we wake up bright and early so Mark and I can begin the drive to Globe. Our first stop will be Globe High School, where I plan to look through the class yearbooks from the 1950s to find the photo of Jean that matches the class photo I have. This will lead me to her maiden name, my holy grail. I'm convinced that today is the day I'll find the clue that will lead me to her.

The backseat holds my arsenal: the photos of Jean and my brother Tommy, my support group notes detailing what to do and what not to do, my "Adopted Child's Memory Book," and last but not least, a photo album filled with my baby photos, as well as photos of my daughters, the granddaughters Jean doesn't know she has. What are the chances I'll find her and be able to show her those albums today? Slim to none. But I bring them along anyway as a beacon of hope.

We drive with all the windows open, and I take in the sights and smells of the desert. The thought that Jean may be breathing this same air, smelling these same smells, and gazing at this same horizon is exciting. Like I'm on a Holy Land pilgrimage, every grain of sand seems to hold significance. Has Jean driven past these landmarks? As I look at people in the surrounding cars, I try to put her photo through age progression in my brain. Does anyone look like her? Even roadside trash takes on significance. Did Jean throw that out there? Yes, it gets weird.

Ninety minutes later, we're driving through Globe, a town of less than 7,000. We find the high school on Main Street with little effort. My eyes absorb the school that I'm sure she attended, and as I climb the steps to the front entrance, I'm filled with awe at the thought that Jean probably climbed these very steps, which signals the fact that I have elevated her to some sort of deity.

We walk through the doors, the bell rings, and students soon crowd the halls. Navigating around them, it will probably come as no surprise that I wonder if I'm related to any of them. I scan the faces rushing past. There's no lightning bolt of recognition with a single one. If I thought I could detect shared DNA through pheromones, like a dog, I might have lifted my nose and sniffed the air.

We enter the office, and I ask the student behind the counter if it would be possible for me to look through their yearbooks from 1952 to 1956. I assume the photo I have is her senior year photo based on the fact that she was twenty-one years old, according to Mom, when she had me. The student nods, leaves the office, and returns with the four books. She allows me to take them out to the front steps to look through them as long as I promise to bring them back.

I head to the doors with the books I'm sure are filled with answers. I take a seat on the top step and, with a deep breath, open the 1956 yearbook, which matches the date on the photo I hold in my hand.

I scan through every photo, starting with the senior class. She's not there. I go through the juniors, sophomores, and freshmen, losing more hope with each class. None of the faces match. Then I try matching names in the back of the book, hoping to find her face in a group shot or candid photo holding pompoms or wearing a homecoming queen crown—anything. My eye scans every "Jean" and the accompanying photos as my confidence sinks lower and lower. I close the book, open another, and repeat. Maybe her photo just didn't make it into this yearbook. My hopes evaporate a little more with each yearbook I close. After the last one, my defeat weighs heavily on my chest as I realize I'm probably not sitting on hallowed ground after all.

Could Jean have gone to this school and never made it into a single yearbook? Not likely. So if Jean never went to

Globe High School, she probably never lived in Globe, not as a high school student anyway.

Then I have an idea. I open the books again and look at the names only. I run my finger down the names looking for Frank Vazquez. Could my birth father be here? He's not.

I'm so disappointed, no make that devastated, as the truth sinks in. I've been so confident I would find Jean's face in these books, and now I have nothing left to go on. How could I have been so certain this was the path I was supposed to take? I never questioned it. Everything depended on a high school yearbook photo. What now?

Mom mentioned that Jean's mother may have worked for the post office. If Jean had never lived here, it's doubtful that her mother did either, but we're here, so the next stop is the Globe Post Office. It's really quite absurd since I don't have a first or last name for Jean's mother. So what am I going to do? Show someone Jean's photo and ask if they recognize her because her mother may have worked there over twenty-five years ago? Find me a straight jacket.

Entering the post office, I feel nothing. No anticipation, no sense of awe or wonder. No ghosts of my ancestors. The "Wanted" posters pinned to the bulletin board hold as much possibility of being a relative. I step up to the counter and say to the clerk, "So this is going to sound a little weird (a little?), but I'm trying to find a friend of my mom's from the fifties. Her name is Jean, and her mom might have worked here back then. Are there any people working here now that may have worked here that long ago?"

"Hold on." She steps around the dividing wall separating the sorting room from the counter. "Wally! Can you come up here a minute?"

A white-haired man with pink cheeks and happy eyes comes around to the front. He reminds me of my dad, and tears threaten as I suppress an overwhelming urge to jump over the counter and hug him.

The clerk asks him, "How long have you worked here? It's been almost forty years, hasn't it?"

"Sure has! Started here right outta high school. Whatcha need?" he replies, approaching the counter.

I repeat the tall tale.

"What was her mother's name?" His logical next question, and wouldn't it have been marvelous if I had *that* answer?

"Unfortunately, I can't remember. But here are some photos of her daughter, Jean, and her son, Tommy. Her married name was Vazquez. Maybe you recognize them?"

He glances at the photos. "She looks familiar, but I don't remember her. You should stop over at Rose Gibson's house. She was a teacher at the high school for thirty-some years. I swear she remembers every student she's ever had. Just go down to the next corner," he says, motioning in a general direction. "Turn right, go past the service station, and it's just up the road apiece. Little yellow house on the left, you can't miss it."

"Thanks, Wally, I really appreciate it."

Exiting the post office, I wonder whether we should waste our time going to Ms. Gibson's house. I've just about eliminated any possibility that Jean ever lived here, but I guess I'm holding onto one thread of hope that Jean may have attended school here for less than a year and might not have made the yearbook. I've certainly got nothing to lose, and, like I said, we're here.

We find the pretty yellow bungalow right where Wally said it would be. We park on the street, walk up to the door, and I knock, heart pounding. Who does this? Surely I'm about to have the door slammed in my face. A woman opens the door, standing all of five feet tall, with gray hair in a bun, and oddly, she seems happy to see us.

"Hello, can I help you?" She smiles at us through the screen door.

"Hi, Ms. Gibson. My name is Amy, and this is my husband, Mark. Wally, over at the Post Office, gave us your name and thought you might be able to help us. I'm looking for an old friend of my mom's who may have been in one of your classes in the fifties."

Without a hint of hesitation, she opens the screen door wide. "Please, call me Rose. C'mon in." She leads us into her living room. "Please sit. How about some lemonade?" and off she goes into the kitchen.

How does this happen? Would I ever be this welcoming to a stranger? It's surreal sitting here in the house of a woman I don't know, in a town I've never been to, waiting for lemonade and hopefully my missing link.

Mark and I sit in silence as I survey the room. It's what I would call a typical grandma's house. Faded flowered wallpaper covers the walls, with white crocheted doilies placed under several framed black-and-white photos. The sun shines through the lace curtains, and I contemplate the absurdities of life while I listen to the ticking of the grandfather clock in the corner. A minute later, Rose returns with a tray of lemonade.

"Here you go. Nothing better than lemonade on a warm day. Now, what's your mother's name?"

"No, not my mother, no, um, a friend of my mother's," I say, sounding a little too panic-stricken at her misunderstanding. I hand her the photo of Jean. "This is the photo of my mom's friend, Jean. I don't know what her last name was."

"Why did you say you were looking for her?" Rose says, taking the photo into her tiny hands bent from arthritis.

The lie I had rehearsed kicks into full throttle, "Well, my mom. . . ." The clock chimes and seems too loud, so I pause as Rose looks closely at the photo. "My mom recently died, and she had always hoped I would meet her best friend someday, so since we're passing through on vacation, I decided to see if I can find her." I say while my heart screams "liar" the whole time my lips are moving.

She looks up with concern, but there's something more in how she looks at me. "I'm so sorry about your mom. What did you say her friend's name was again?"

My heart sinks. I know repeating her name isn't going to help. "It's Jean."

"Jean. Jean. She does look familiar," Rose says, almost under her breath as she continues to study the photo.

"What's your mom's name? Did I have her in class, too?" she asks, looking up from the photo. Again, I feel like she's looking right through me. My mom's name—I hadn't planned for that question. So stupid. Blood rushes to my head. Is my deer-in-the-headlights look ratting me out?

"Oh, Sally . . . Sally Smith."

Smith. Really, Amy? Why not Jane Doe? I stink at lying. I watch her as if she's trying to pull a distant memory out of the shadows.

"Sally Smith, I don't remember that name either. I'm pretty good at remembering all the students I've had. Classes were pretty small back then, so that helps." She pauses, handing me back the photo. "Well, I'm no spring chicken anymore, so maybe my memory is slipping a little." She giggles.

I feel horrible for making this precious little woman feel like she's losing it. Actually, I feel horrible about the whole thing, period. We spend the next hour listening to Rose's stories, including why she's never married (her students came first), why she loves Globe (she was born here and will die here), and all about her cat, Dinah, named after the cat in *Alice in Wonderland. (*which is perfect since I'm pretty sure I've fallen through the rabbit hole, and I'm just sitting here waiting for the cat to smile. No, wait, it's the Cheshire Cat who smiles. Whatever. Dinah might as well smile, too).

I feel disconnected as Mark laughs and talks with her. I'm thankful he's here to do that while I smile, nod, and try to listen while all I really want to do is cry. What do I do now? I've pinned all my hopes on Globe, but now it's just a little town with a big name that's filled with friendly people. My mind spins as I try to pull together any other options I may not have considered.

I've got nothing.

As the conversation wanes, I suddenly stand. "Well, thank you, Rose, for your hospitality. We don't want to take up any more of your time, and we've got to get going." I realize I could have eased into that exit stage right a little more graciously, so I smile and add what I genuinely feel, "And don't you worry, you're not losing your memory. I've probably got things mixed up, and they may never have attended school here." The only thing left to do is curtsey, but thankfully, I come to my senses and give Rose a hug instead.

"I'm so sorry I couldn't help you, dear."

"No, Rose, thank you. You've been very kind."

It's over. It's all over. That's the only thought I have as I walk to the car with that yearbook photo in my hand and a concrete vat of emptiness that has taken the place of my stomach. The questions and hopes I've accumulated have been extinguished in less than five hours. The October sun feels too bright and too hot, and the few steps to the car feel like a mile. I'm melting, but more on the inside than out. No words are spoken as we enter the car. I clarify that I'm in no mood for conversation with my single-word answers in reply to Mark's attempts at conversation. It's going to be a long drive back to his sister's house. I'm in full-blown pout mode, with my face turned away. I look out my window but see nothing while holding back the tears. It's no one's fault. Maybe this is the way it's supposed to end.

Mark suddenly yanks the car left, turning into the Chamber of Commerce parking lot. "Geez, what are you doing?" I ask, knocked out of my stupor, adding insult to the mood I'm already in.

"Maybe we can pick up some brochures for things to do in the area since we've got six more days here," he replies, pulling into a parking spot. I interpret his statement as an official declaration of the end of my search. He may as well have said, "Well, that's over. Now, let's have a vacation." I could assume his quest for travel brochures is his way to distract my grief and lift the black cloud that's settled over my head. But I know he probably just wants to escape the suffocating silence of the car. It doesn't really matter. My reply would be the same, “I don’t need any brochures. This isn’t a vacation. I’m here to find my birth mother.”

“Fine, sit here in the car then. I’m going in.”

“Fine.”

And that’s precisely what happens. Like an insolent five-year-old, I sit, and as I sit, the car gets hotter as it usually does in Arizona with its never-ending sunshine. I’m soon reminded of that glass of Rose’s lemonade. It’s only been minutes since I started my vacation strike, and now I have to humble myself and enter the vacation zone to find a bathroom.

I exit the car, slamming the door with the appropriate amount of force to signal that I’m irritated—a pointless effort since I’m alone in this empty parking lot in the middle of the desert. I yank open the door to the building with just the right amount of flourish that I hope will sufficiently display my air of irritation and vacation defiance. The effort is, again, wasted. Mark doesn’t look up from the rack of brochures.

A lady wearing a name tag that says “Nancy” looks up from her magazine. “Hello, can I help you?”

“Hello. Thank you, no. I just need to use your restroom.” I try not to mumble while scraping up some semblance of a smile for her as I walk past Mark in silence, still maintaining my annoyance at his unilateral annulment of my search. He ignores my presence completely. Whatever. I figure when I’m done, I’ll just get the keys from him so I can turn on the air conditioning in the car and then make my dramatic exit from the building. When I exit the restroom, however, I hear Mark and Nancy talking. Of course, they are. Mark can hold a conversation with a turnip.

" . . . had hoped she could meet her, but no luck." Mark says, turning towards me and asking, "Do you have the photo of Jean with you? Nancy grew up here and went to Globe High School in the fifties. Maybe she'll recognize her."

I pull the yearbook photo out of my pocket and hand it to Nancy. "What's her last name?" Nancy asks.

And now I have to talk. Fantastic. *What a fabulous waste of time* is all I can think. "Her married name was Vazquez, but my mom said she divorced in the late fifties or early sixties, so I'm not sure what it would be today. Unfortunately, I can't remember her maiden name."

Nancy looks at the photo, and like Rose, I feel she sees through the story we've told, so I keep talking, hoping it will stop her brain from processing the lie. "My mom told me Jean's husband's name was Frank, and her son's name was Tommy."

"I don't remember her."

Big surprise.

She continues, "But I have a lot of friends in the area, so I'll ask around. Can you give me a number where I can reach you if I hear anything?"

Mark gives Nancy his sister's phone number as I thank her. My thanks are heartfelt. I can't get over how helpful everyone has been, even if it has yielded no results. We're walking out the door, with Mark clutching his travel brochures, when Nancy says, "Oh, and you should try the Family Search Library run by the Church of Latter-Day Saints down in Mesa. They have a lot of genealogical information there that might help you locate your mom's friend."

My hopes ignite at one more glimmer of possibility. "Thank you so much, Nancy!" I say with more enthusiasm than I've had in the last three hours.

Getting into the car, Mark says, "To the Family Search Library?" and just like that, my inner brat slinks back to her cozy corner, where she curls up on her throne of sulks and tantrums, grumbling about how she was totally robbed of her moment to shine. Gone for now, but she'll be back, I'm sure.

When we arrive, the library is closed. We'll have to come back tomorrow. At the end of it all, Day One (has it really only been a day?) was pretty much a bust. The only things we got out of it were the knowledge that Jean never went to school in Globe, a tip about the search library, and some travel brochures.

I call Mom and Dad to check on the girls and give them my update. They continue to encourage me and say that tomorrow may be the day. It only makes me realize even more how much I love them. I miss my daughters terribly and I talk to them as they get ready for bed.

It seems I underestimated how emotionally draining this trip would be. I go from chastising myself for being so naïve, thinking I could find Jean with nothing more than a first name and a photo, to feeling sorry for myself. I try my best not to be a downer at dinner, but it seems all my energy has left me, and I can't eat, so I go to bed early. As I lie in bed, alone in the dark, I resign myself to the fact that I may not find Jean. That's when I again feel urged to pray —from the depths of my soul it comes.

"It's me again, God. I've done everything I can to find Jean, and I've come to a dead end. I know it's not a surprise to You that I'm out of clues. Is this You telling me to stop and be thankful for what I have and what You've given me? If I don't get another clue, I'll take that as a sign that You don't want me to find her, and I'll accept that and try never to think about it again. But, God, if You want me to find her, I need one more clue. Thank You for everything in my life and all that You've done for me." Peace washes over me. My face is wet. I never even felt the tears falling.

Smokestack Revelations

The next day, I wake up feeling refreshed and in a much better frame of mind. I even look over the travel brochures at breakfast as we plan how to spend the rest of the week. I know, hard to believe. We will, of course, visit the Family Search Library this morning, but in my mind, it's just a formality. I've given it to God and tell myself there's a reason for everything, and I'm truly okay with my search ending right here, right now.

As we're getting ready to walk out the door, the phone rings, and my sister-in-law answers. "Yes, she's right here. Can I tell her who's calling?" She turns to hand me the phone. "It's for you. She says her name is Nancy."

Nancy. Chamber of Commerce Nancy?

I take the receiver. "Hello?"

"Hi Amy, this is Nancy. We met yesterday at the Chamber of Commerce?"

"Oh, yes!" My answer sounds too loud as my heart leaps in my chest.

“I spoke to one of my friends last night, and she suggested you check Superior. She said a Vazquez family lived there in the fifties and she thinks some of the family are still living there.”

If I could jump through the phone and hug her, I would, but instead, I thank her and hang up, our plans instantly changed. Postponing our trip to the Family Search Library, we begin our drive to Superior as we did the day before, with a map in my lap and my baby album on the back seat. As the landscape rushes by, I close my eyes and ask, “God, is this that one more clue I asked You for?”

Looking at the map, I see we passed through Superior on our way to Globe yesterday, but I never gave it much more than a glance. Once again, excitement fills me, but this time I’m able to keep it in check. I know what it feels like to have my hopes shattered.

As we approach Superior, my eyes take in the red rock hills and the old copper mine, and then my heart stops. No, really, I think it actually stops for a couple of seconds because there in the middle of town is a smokestack. I reach over the seat, grab the folder of photos from the back seat, and pull out a photo, holding it up to the windshield. The photo showing Jean sitting on a car bumper and holding Tommy in her lap with a smokestack in the background. Could this be that smokestack? My eyes travel between the photo and the smokestack. It looks exactly the same, including the hills surrounding it. We passed this smokestack yesterday, twice in fact, on our way to Globe and on our return, but I never noticed it. How did I not see it?

"I found her," I whisper, barely containing my excitement, but for the sake of my sanity, I really have to rein it in. I tell myself that even if this is where Jean is from and I find her maiden name, there's still no guarantee I'll be able to find her. But I now have something tangible that connects her to this place, so no matter how I try to convince myself not to get my hopes up, they are as high as they could possibly be. And then there's my prayer. If this is God's clue, how can it not lead me to her?

Superior has less than half the population of Globe. The town is old, like some old ghost town in a Western movie. I try to picture it as the more vibrant town I imagine it was when Jean lived here —if she lived here. Whether or not she lived here, I know she was here at least long enough to take that photo. I'm looking at houses that probably look exactly like they did back then. They all look old. We drive slowly through the little downtown area, passing boarded-up shops and an old abandoned movie theater. Did Jean ever watch movies there or maybe even work there? I look at every building in awe and imagine I'm seeing them through her eyes. First, we'll find the high school and then drive around and see if I can figure out where this photo was taken.

With the windows open, I inhale deeply as thoughts flood my mind, including one that ends with her no longer being alive. I push that thought aside, though I also know if there's a cemetery, we'll stop there too. I marvel that she must have driven on this same little road down Main Street. It's the only one running through town.

Then I see it—the old two-story, red brick high school sitting on top of a hill, and once again, Mark and I are climbing high school steps that feel like holy ground. I pull open the door and enter the front office. It smells musty like every old school does. The lobby is small, and photos of the most recent graduates line the walls. Above them, a plaque reads "Class of 1984." I walk around the room, looking at the photos and reading the names below them while waiting for my turn at the counter. I come to a photo of a girl named Sara. It catches my eye because her last name, Zacatenco, is unique and the same last name as my dad's good friend, Tony. He and my dad, both retired Navy men, golf together every week. I'll have to remember to tell Dad about seeing Tony's family name here, in this tiny little town.

Finally, it's my turn, and the student behind the counter looks at me expectantly but doesn't say a word.

"I'm wondering if I can see your class yearbooks from the fifties?" I ask.

"All our yearbooks from back then burned in a fire," she says nonchalantly. She doesn't know that she just extinguished all my hopes with a single sentence.

This. Can't. Be. Happening. I feel the color drain from my face while sounds are suddenly muffled. All I can hear is the ringing in my ears like someone has put a bucket over my head. The last time I felt this way, I passed out.

I stand there in awkward silence without a single thought when a door bearing a brass plate that says "Principal" opens. A silver-haired woman walks out and up to the counter. I feel pale, and I must look that way because she asks me, with concern in her voice, "Is everything okay?"

I don't answer because nothing is okay, and I've suddenly forgotten how to speak.

"Can I help you?" Her second question.

If I don't answer now, she may call the police. Why isn't Mark speaking? My throat feels as though it has closed up, so I reply in a voice that's an octave higher than it should be, "I was hoping to look at your yearbooks from the fifties, but I hear they all burned."

"Well, yes, that's true. Is there something in those books you need?"

"I'm looking for a friend of my mom's who went to school here and I can't remember her last name but my mom has always wanted me to meet her so while we were in the area I figured I would stop by and see if anyone remembers her and knows where she is because my mom died and really wanted me to meet her best friend so anyway I was hoping to find her in your yearbooks." One long, run-on, incoherent sentence, and for the first time since I started telling this tall tale, it now feels so full of holes that I wonder what I was thinking. I finally stop talking and lay the little yearbook photo of Jean on the counter in front of her.

She picks it up. "Why, that looks like Jean Hawkins."

I must have misheard her. Did she say, "Jean?" But I don't ask; I just watch her as I now feel like I'm underwater and everything is moving in slow motion. She turns and walks over to a gray five-drawer file cabinet and pulls open a drawer. Thumbing through the many folders stuffed inside, she pulls out a single folder and lays it on the counter in front of me. When she opens it, she turns it around to face me, and there, stapled to the top of the inside cover, are four yearbook photos of Jean, one for each high school year, including the last one that matches the photo I hold in my hand.

"Come on back to my office," she says as she takes the folder, opens a little gate, and motions Mark and me to enter the room behind the counter. I turn to Mark and ask him to run out to the car to get my notebook. I have a feeling I'll be writing things down. Following this woman into her office,

I'm pretty sure my heart is about to explode as she smiles and closes the door behind her. She offers her hand to shake mine. "I'm Betty, and you are?"

"Amy," I squeak.

She motions to a chair as she sits down behind her desk. "Have a seat."

I sit down and swallow, trying to clear my throat, willing my voice to return to normal.

"And now, you can tell me, this is your mother, isn't it?"

How am I still conscious right now with all the air sucked out of the room? The throbbing in my head has to be making my eyeballs pulse in and out of my skull. My face feels like it's on fire, and I know the big red blotches that always appear when I'm nervous have sprouted and are spreading across my neck and chest. I also know that all these reactions are giving away my secret. There is no way I can't hide the fact that this is not some.casual visit to a school that will lead me to my mom's "friend." I'm clearly much more emotionally invested than the lie I have every intention of telling. The proverbial cat is out of the bag, yet I try.

"No, it's an old friend of my mother's." I feel the sweat breaking out on the back of my neck.

"Honey—look in the mirror! You're the spitting image of her!" Betty says with a smile that takes up her entire face.

Like fireworks going off in the room, I instantly understand why every single person has said Jean looks familiar and why every gaze at my face made me think they were seeing more. They were. My resemblance to my birth mother is, in one word, uncanny. What was I thinking?

I cave. I mean, what else can I do? Here I sit with a woman who knows Jean, or knew her anyway, and has presented me with exactly what I've been looking for. How can I be anything but honest with her?

"Okay, yes, Jean is my birth mother. All the rules say not to tell our birth mother's secret, so I was trying to honor that. I was adopted at birth, and I'm trying to find her, but I don't know if she would even want that or if she would want anyone to know. I don't know if she's married, has other children, or even if she's alive. But if I'm a secret, I really don't want to cause her any problems." The release of the truth is like a weight lifting, and I let out a slow exhale.

A knock at her door. It's Mark with my notebook.

I introduce him to Betty, and then I tell him, "She knows Jean is my birth mother."

He smiles, sits down, and asks, "Is that a good thing?"

"Well, I think it is," Betty says and then continues, "I can tell you that your mother is very much alive, as far as I know. Last I heard, she's living in Phoenix, and her mother, Mae, lives with her. In fact, Jean's brother, Ronny, lived here in Superior until just a few months ago. He moved his family to Montana after his youngest daughter graduated. Let me see, I should have his number," Betty keeps talking as she thumbs through her Rolodex.

This small-town life I've seen on display over the last two days amazes me. I feel like I'm sitting in Mayberry, just waiting for Andy and Barney to walk in. My high school graduating class had over 700 students. I can't even remember my principal's name, and he's not likely to remember any student who attended there over twenty years ago unless maybe the student had been a sports star, valedictorian, or had set fire to the building or something.

"Yes, here it is." She writes the phone number on a piece of paper and hands it to me. "Your uncle should be able to tell you where your mother is or at least give you her phone number."

My uncle. Those words seep in. My uncle! I take the slip of paper from her as if it's a fragile butterfly. "Thank you so much, Betty." I'm trying not to cry—again. We stand, and she comes around the desk to hug me. She'll never know how important she has just become to my story.

"You're very welcome. I hope it all turns out just the way you want it to."

As I walk to the door clutching that piece of paper like I've found the holy grail, I turn and say, "Oh, and you won't tell anyone, right?" because I have to make sure. I have, after all, broken all the rules.

"Of course not," Betty nods, reassuring me with a smile.

Getting into the car, I think about how close I am to finding Jean—like maybe one call away. No, make that two calls. First, I have to call my uncle. It just got very real. No longer looking in awe at the surroundings, I look for a pay phone as we drive down the hill.

"Don't you want to wait till we get home to call him?" Mark asks.

"I have to call now," I say, pointing to a telephone booth outside a small grocery market. I enter the store to get change for the pay phone. Now that I know Jean has probably been here, my hand lingers a little longer than normal on the old grocery store door handle, and I examine every detail of this little store like I'm looking at it through her eyes and smelling it with her nose.

Back at the payphone, I dial the number. My heart is taking a beating this trip for sure.

"Hello?" It's the voice of a teenage boy.

"Hi, is Ronny there?" I ask, hoping he can't hear the pounding in my chest.

"Just a minute . . . Daaaad! Phone!" He yells as the receiver is clunked down on a hard surface. This is my cousin, who will forever hold the honor of being the first of my birth family I've ever spoken to, a fact he may never know.

The receiver is picked up. "Hello," Ronny answers matter-of-factly. Not like a hello with a question mark, but more like a "Hello-it's-me-say-what-you-called-to-say." He has what I can only describe as a cowboy drawl.

"Hi, Ronny." I pause just a second. I can't tell him who I really am. Jean has to be the first to know. "This is Sally." That name on the back of Jean's yearbook photo. I mean, why not? "I went to school with your sister, Jean. I'm visiting Arizona and stopped at our old high school to reminisce. I couldn't believe Betty is still the principal. Anyway, she gave me your number and told me you might have Jean's number."

I'm satisfied with my theatrical performance, but then there's a pause on the other end of the line, and for just a second, I panic. Could Ronny have known Jean's friend, Sally? What if she was his old girlfriend? These thoughts invade my brain at warp speed, and I instantly regret picking a name he might know.

But then he speaks, “Hi, Sally. I haven’t talked to Jean in a while, but I know she’s living over there in Phoenix with Mom. Hold on a minute, and I’ll get her number."

I’m relieved and excited. Relieved that he didn’t ask “Sally” how she was doing or if she remembered him from school. But more than anything, I’m excited. I have just found Jean and her brother sounds like a normal person, so maybe she is, too. He’s back on the line, reading off Jean’s phone number as I write it down.

“Thanks, Ronny. I really appreciate it.”

“You’re welcome.”

“Have a nice day.” Have a nice day? Shut up, Amy, and hang up the phone.

“You too, Sally.”

As we start the drive back to my sister-in-law’s house, I can’t take my eyes off the smokestack that I completely missed the day before. How did I overlook something so obvious? Then it hits me—the real question is not how but why did I miss it? It’s as if I had to come to the end of myself to realize I needed God’s help. The answer to that desperate prayer has made me see God’s hand in this whole thing, and with that realization, my eyes can’t hold back the tears.

As the events of the day play over and over in my head, there are so many things I wish I’d asked Betty. What kind of girl was Jean? Did she belong to any clubs? If Jean hangs up on me, I'm returning to ask Betty all those questions and get copies of all her other school photos stapled to that folder.

I sit with my eyes closed, leaning back on the seat as thoughts flood my mind. The call I'm about to make will either mark the beginning or the end. Either way, God's will is about to be done, and there's great peace in that. I'm so very thankful.

Moment of Truth

I've looked at my notes and practiced what I'm going to say at least a dozen times. I go to the bedroom alone to make the call. I know that's terribly unfair to Mark since he's been through all of this with me, but I can't bear the thought of anyone seeing my disappointment if Jean hangs up on me. As much as I tell myself I'm okay either way, I'm not, and I dread the disappointment of being rejected again.

I pace the bedroom with the now familiar sound of blood rushing in my ears as I work up the courage to actually dial the phone. The doubts are like a tidal wave of flooding thoughts. *How will I really feel if she doesn't want to talk to me? What if she gets mad? What if she doesn't even remember me? What if? What if? What if?* I'm starting to hate those two words. I can't even imagine the scenario of her being happy to hear from me. My hands are shaking as I dial the number, and I can feel the hives breaking out on my chest and neck again. I'm thankful she can't see me. How am I going to get her to take down my number before she hangs up on me?

It's ringing. *What am I doing?* I could still hang up. Then a voice answers—a voice that sounds too old to be Jean. This is my grandmother. I'm speaking to my grandmother.

"Hello?"

"Hello, is Jean there?"

"No, I'm sorry, she's not. She's at the doctor. Can I take a message or have her call you back?"

She sounds kind. Not at all like the larger-than-life Viking woman in an opera wearing a horned helmet that I've pictured all my life. She was, after all, the reason Jean couldn't keep me. At least that's what I've told myself all these years because it was always easier than believing my birth mother didn't want me. But all that evaporates when I hear her voice.

"No, that's okay. I'll call back later." And I hang up quickly without even hearing her response. Why is Jean at the doctor? I close my eyes and pray, "Dear God, please don't let her have heart issues."

Wouldn't that be something? I tell her who I am, and she falls over dead. This imagination of mine can be a curse. I'll call back again after dinner as if I could actually eat anything. Dinner tonight is so different from the night before. Tonight, I'm filled with excitement and a touch of dread versus last night's dinner, which was filled with life-sucked-out-of-me disappointment. I will hear my birth mother's voice before I go to sleep tonight.

I take my time calling back. I don't want to interrupt her dinner, but mostly because I don't want to interrupt her life, nor do I relish facing the agony of my defeat. It becomes clear that I'm stalling when Mark asks if I've decided to wait till tomorrow to call.

"No, I'll call now," I say as I return to the bedroom phone, close the door, wipe my sweaty palms on my pants, and dial the number.

It's ringing. Once. Twice. Three times.

Then a voice that sounds very much like my own, just like it says it may in my notes, answers the phone. It's her. There is no doubt in my mind.

"Hello?"

"Hello, is this Jean?" I can't believe any words at all are coming out of my mouth.

"Yes, it is." She sounds nice.

Now comes the hard part. Getting her to take down my phone number.

"Hi, Jean. This is a really important phone call. Can you take down my number in case we get disconnected?" I hear what sounds like a roaring ocean in my ears. Now, the only question I have is whether I will pass out before or after she hangs up on me.

"Sure, just a minute."

Wait, what? Just like that, she's going to take down my number? Why would she do that with a complete stranger calling? For the record, I would never take down your number without asking you twenty-seven questions. I can't believe it.

She's back, "Okay, go ahead."

I panic. What is the number I'm calling from? I hadn't really thought I would get this far. Stupid. Then I remember the phone number is printed on a piece of paper under a plastic cover on the phone. I read off the number. And now for the moment of truth. I can almost hear the drumroll in my head as I take another deep breath and say, "So, I'm wondering, does February 27, 1959, mean anything to you?"

Can she hear the hope in my voice? Does she think I sound like her, too? Nothing but silence. How long have I been holding my breath?

"No?" Jean replies quietly. Not a statement, but more like a question awaiting further explanation.

So this is it, the moment it all ends. The moment I was expecting. She's going to deny that I'm hers. My heart begins to crack as it sinks. The feeling that I'm going to pass out is replaced with the feeling that I'm going to throw up, but I try to hold back the disappointment in my voice. "Oh, okay . . . well . . . um . . . does the name Amy Robin mean anything to you?" I try to sound nonchalant, giving her my name despite the heart-wrenching disappointment I'm feeling over her not recognizing my birth date.

Then she says—nothing.

My heart is beating so hard it actually hurts. Maybe I'm the one who's going to have the heart attack. Really, can a heart explode? I feel like it might right now. I wait to hear the click of the phone being hung up. It's surely coming. I know this is the woman who gave birth to me. Is it possible that she has forgotten everything about me? The day I was born, the name she gave me, or that I even exist at all? Or is she now replaying the moment of my birth or the last time she saw me? Is her heart racing as fast as mine is? Does she remember the name my parents had picked out for her child? If she does remember, is she afraid? Afraid that her secret is going to be revealed to her husband, her children, and the world? Or has she blocked it all from her mind? Could the heartache of giving a child away create amnesia as a self-defense mechanism? She's either weighing her options or has put me so far out of her mind that I have ceased to exist for her. Maybe a part of her really did die of a broken heart. How can all these thoughts be tripping over each other in my head? How long have I been waiting in the silence? Was I so engrossed in my thoughts that I missed the sound of her hanging up the phone? But no, I still hear her television playing in the background.

Then I hear her, barely, "Yes."

Did she say yes? She did! She said, "YES!" She remembers my name. My eyes fill with tears. I haven't practiced what to say next.

"Well, this is Amy and . . . well, I just wanted to thank you."

Without hesitation, she asks, "Thank me for what?" Her voice sounds heavy. Is that sarcasm? No, it's something that sounds, I don't know, irritated? No, wait, not irritated—guilty. If guilt had a sound, this would be it.

"For having me. You didn't have to do that, and I wanted you to know I'm very thankful," I say with complete sincerity. That's it, isn't it? That's what I feel for her. It's not love, exactly. It's undying, pure, unadulterated gratitude for the sacrifice she made to give me life, and I'm hoping she'll believe me.

Her silence feels ominous to me as if she's feeling backed onto the edge of a cliff and is trying to decide where to go from here. I feel like I have to fill the silence with something to keep her from jumping off the precipice and hanging up. So I continue with words that seem to tumble out of my mouth in rapid succession. "I just want you to know that I'm happy and healthy, and I don't need anything from you, like money or anything. I only wanted you to know that I'm alive and okay. I really don't want to cause you any trouble, and if you don't want anyone to know, I won't tell."

Am I saying the right words? *Please don't hang up on me. Please don't jump.*

"Where are you?" The heaviness in her voice is gone.

"Oh, I'm over here at my sister-in-law's house." That's it. That's my silly, mindless response. Now she'll think I'm playing riddles with her, but my mind is suddenly blank. I have no roadmap for this part of the trip.

"And where is that?" Do I hear her smiling?

"Oh, Mesa. I live in Illinois, but we came here to visit my sister-in-law." Which is not really the whole truth, is it? I didn't come to Arizona to visit my sister-in-law; I came here for one reason only—to find HER. But I don't want her to know yet how important this is to me, how important she is to me. Like holding onto this little tidbit protects me from the possibility of getting hurt.

"I'd like to see you," she says, and just like that, the door opens and swings wide. My birth mother would like to see me. She isn't going to hang up. The clouds part, and the angels sing.

"You would?" I ask, unable to hide my surprise as big black dots float before my eyes. I may be hyperventilating. *Slow breaths, Amy. Slow.* "I'd like that. I don't know your situation, and again, I don't want to cause you any trouble. I can meet you anywhere. " I stop myself as I feel a ramble coming on and simply say, "Anywhere would be great."

I hear her voice, muffled as she puts her hand over the receiver, "Mom, it's my daughter. She wants to meet me. Should I have her come here or meet her somewhere else?"

Then I hear the distant voice of my grandmother. "My God, child, that's my granddaughter. Have her come here!"

"Can you come to my house in Phoenix?"

"Now?"

"Yes."

"I'd like that!" Did I sound too excited? *Calm down, Amy*. I jot down the address and get directions. "Okay. See you soon."

I just said "See you soon" to my birth mother. What alternate reality have I fallen into? Is this really happening, or am I going to wake up? Please don't let this be a dream.

I bound out of the bedroom. Okay, bound may be strong, but I'm clearly excited as I recount the call with Mark and his sister, who are sitting in the kitchen and, for all I know, overheard my side of the conversation. I have to get ready. Shower, change, and put on my makeup. I have to make a great first impression. I feel like it's the most important first date I've ever had. It's Thursday, October 4, 1984, and I'm meeting my birth mother for the first time—or second time if being born counts.

When Truth Crashes the Party

Mark drives the dark roads while I read off the directions Jean provided to her home. We don't say much as I take in the surrounding landscape, with thoughts swirling in my head. We turn down her street and slow as we approach the house, a modest avocado-green, single-story home with a carport in one of the older neighborhoods. Then I see her, standing in the driveway, tall, thin, bleached-blonde, and smoking a cigarette. I suddenly wish I hadn't dyed my hair.

Jean was twenty-one years old when she gave birth to me, according to my mom. That would make her about forty-six years old now and the same age my mom was when she adopted me. Coincidence? Or is God showing me again that He's right here? I open the car door and quickly walk towards her as she walks towards me. We wrap our arms around each other, and she says, "I knew my God would bring you back to me." She has no idea how true that statement is.

We stand in that embrace while it feels like the earth has stopped turning, and then she takes my hand and leads me to the front door. Grandma Mae, who undoubtedly was watching out the window, opens the door. She looks nothing like the caricature of her I had created. She's a little shorter than I am, with white hair and a kind, smiling face. I have a grandmother.

We sit down in the living room, which is lined with paintings on the walls signed "Jean." So, this is where I get my artistic gene. Jean takes my face in her hands and turns it towards her, saying, "You have your father's eyes." My father. I didn't think we'd get to that topic so quickly.

"Is he still around? My father?" Might I actually be able to meet both of my birth parents? How wonderful would that be?

"I don't know," Jean replies. "I didn't know him very well."

Those few words confuse me, and my thoughts do somersaults. "What do you mean?" is what I want to ask, but nothing comes out of my mouth, which is okay as she continues.

"I met your father at my sister's graduation party and only spent that one night with him. I remember his name was Charles Neal. He was tall and so good-looking, with dark hair and piercing blue eyes. He was a friend of my cousin's. They both worked in the copper mines."

"Do you have any photos of him?" I ask hopefully.

"No. I'm sorry."

"Not even one?" as if asking this will jog her memory of one she's hidden somewhere.

"Not even one. There wasn't time," which is awkward enough for a chuckle. Literally, a chuckle, a sound I didn't even know I could make. Jean smiles as she searches my face to see if she can decipher how I'm really feeling about this revelation that I'm the result of a one-night stand.

"Did he know about me? Did you ever see him again to tell him you were pregnant?"

"Yes, I went to the place he was living and told him I was pregnant. He laughed when I told him. I don't think he believed me. That was the last time I ever spoke to him. I don't think he ever knew whether or not you were born."

This is a totally unexpected revelation, and I ask, "Do you have any idea where he is now?"

"No."

"What about your cousin who was friends with him? Would he know?"

"I'm estranged from that part of the family. I don't even know where my cousin is."

It feels like this topic of discussion is over, though I have so many questions that seem logical. For one, isn't there someone in the family who knows where this cousin is? There has to be. Maybe it's something we can come back to later or someday.

But what if my birth father forever remains a mystery? How do I feel about that? I find I'm a little more disappointed than I thought I would be since I've barely given him a thought over my lifetime other than wondering about medical information or possible siblings.

The story I've been told all my life didn't include this information, and I can only surmise it's because Jean never told Mom and Dad the real reason she was getting a divorce. I must have been the reason. I've always thought Tommy and I shared the same father. A father who seemingly had no issue with divorcing his wife, who was carrying his child, and didn't even care enough to provide support, as the story goes, so I wrote him off. It seems I've filled in some of the blanks with faulty data. Jean, however, gave me nine months of her life. She kept herself healthy for my benefit, felt me growing and moving inside her, and then went through childbirth only to say "Goodbye." She's the one who matters most to me right now, so I change direction.

"So, how is Tommy?" I ask. "Do you still call him Tommy?"

Jean's demeanor instantly changes. Smiling, no, make that glowing, she laughs. "He's Tom now. He's twenty-seven and lives in the Bahamas. In fact, he's coming home for a visit next week."

Darn. Missed him by a week, but maybe that's for the best.

"I knew about Tom," I say as I take out the four photos that I've been showing to strangers around Arizona and hand them to her. She takes the photos and gets up to get her glasses, which are lying on a table next to a recliner. When she puts the glasses on, I gasp. "We have the same glasses!" I exclaim, taking my glasses out of my purse to prove it to her. My excitement about this small coincidence is palpable. I've never had something like this happen, and it feels much more significant than simply eyeglass frames, like my first inherited attraction to the same thing.

"We do!" She seems almost as excited as I am, and we laugh.

Looking at the photos, she says, "These are the photos I gave your mom to give you!"

"They gave them to me when I was eleven years old. They had that yearbook photo enlarged, and it's been sitting on my bedroom dresser ever since. It's the yearbook photo that helped me find you. I didn't have your maiden name, but Dad said he thought you were from Globe. So I went to Globe yesterday and looked through the yearbooks at the school but couldn't find you."

Was that only yesterday? It feels like forever-ago. I continue with my story, telling her about our time in Globe and Superior and ending with Principal Betty at Superior High School. Grandma Mae, who has been listening intently and quietly while seated next to me on the sofa, finally speaks, laughing. "You asked Betty not to tell anyone, but you may as well have shouted it out the window. That woman could never keep a secret." We all laugh. I'll later discover that silence is not the norm for my very talkative grandma.

Still looking at the photos, Jean says, "I also gave your mom a doll wearing a wedding dress to give to you. Did you get that?"

I replay in my mind all the old photos in the photo albums Mom has made for me. "No, I don't remember a doll in a wedding dress."

Jean seems disappointed but goes on. "You were conceived right under that smokestack," Jean says, pointing to the photo of the smokestack. I wanted answers, but this was not one of them, and I'm not sure how I should respond to that little tidbit.

Sensing the slightly awkward moment of silence, Jean declares, "Well, maybe that was a little too much information." She laughs, and I, in relief, laugh with her.

Changing direction, I tell her a little about me, though she hasn't asked any questions about my life yet. "So, you have two granddaughters." I say, handing her their photos, and we spend the next ten minutes with me showing her their photos and telling her all about them, ending with, "I can't wait for you to meet them!"

Both Jean and Grandma do a respectable amount of "oooing" and "ahhhing." Then Grandma uses the lull in conversation to get up and tells Mark, "Let's you and I go into the other room and give them a little privacy," and off they go. Jean then gets up from the sofa and takes two framed photos from the shelf. She hands me one.

"This is your brother, Tom," she says. Pictured is a handsome man with long, wavy black hair and olive skin—the man whose baby photo has sat on my dresser for fourteen years. Tommy.

"And this is your brother, Danny. He's a year and a half younger than you." I take the photo from her. Brown curly hair, blue eyes, and a face that looks so much like mine, it's hard to believe we don't share a father.

"Do they know about me?" I ask, secretly hoping they do.

"No, I never told them. I was always afraid of what they would think of me. But now, well, I have to figure out how to tell them, and I hope they don't hate me for keeping it from them."

For the first time, I feel like a secret. Jean senses my disappointment and says, "Anyone I've ever dated or married has known about you, though. I always hoped there was a chance I'd get you back, and I wanted them to know."

A chance I'd get you back. The statement shakes me, but I don't have time to dwell on it as she goes on, "I've been married four times. Well, three, really, since I was married to Danny's dad twice."

"Wow." I instantly regret using that word.

"I know. Embarrassing, right? I guess I'm not very good at being married. I've been dating a guy for a few years now, and he left for Mexico this morning. In fact, when you called, I thought it might be someone calling to tell me he's cheating on me again, maybe down in Mexico with another woman. That's why I took down your number when you asked me to. Otherwise, I'd have probably just hung up." See? I wasn't wrong; it was weird that she took down my number. But then I think, there's God again. If I'd called yesterday or any other day, this might have ended differently.

"Cheating on you again?" I ask with emphasis on the again part. "I've always been a one-and-done kinda girl when it comes to a guy cheating on me," I say, thinking she might not be very good at dating either.

"Yeah, I know. I keep telling myself that."

Changing the subject, I ask, "All these years, I thought that Tommy, I mean Tom, and I had the same father."

"Frank was Tom's dad. We dated from the time I was twelve, if you can call it dating when you're twelve. We got married when I was seventeen. He was Mexican. Tom looks a lot like him."

Surely my eyes aren't as big as they feel. "You're not going to believe this, but my first boyfriend from the time I was twelve years old was Mexican, and we got married when I was seventeen, too!" It's hard to describe how these coincidences make me feel connected to her, and she shares my excitement and surprise at how similar many of our experiences have been.

"Wow. Really? That's quite a coincidence, isn't it?" She continues, "Well, Frank was the love of my life. He was in the Navy, and I didn't see him very much. Tom and I were living in California, where Frank was stationed, and that's when I met your mom and dad. They managed the small apartment complex where we lived and were always so nice to us. Anyway, Frank was gone a lot with the Navy, and one of these times, Tom and I went back home to Superior for my sister's high school graduation party. Your father, Charles, came to the party with my cousin, and one thing led to another and, well, you know. Anyway, it wasn't until I was almost three months along that I realized I was pregnant, and I was terrified. I didn't know what to do. Since Frank had been away, I obviously couldn't say the baby was his, and I knew if I told him what had happened, it would be the end of our marriage."

She pauses. Her voice changes, becoming thicker somehow, "I really loved him" A long pause. "He died in a car accident in 1962."

I haven't blinked as I sit awestruck at what I'm hearing. "Anyway, my friends all told me it would be easier to end it, you know? They gave me all kinds of suggestions that might help, like taking a really hot bath and jumping off the refrigerator. They said if that didn't work, they knew someone who could take care of it. No one would ever have to know, especially Frank. Life could just go on as usual."

She pauses here and I can see she's lost in the memory, while I suddenly see those black spots again. The soft, smooth words she says instantly transform into words with sharp edges that pierce my heart. "It would be easier to end it," they said. The "it" was me. It was just a casual discussion amongst friends about ending my life so her life could "just go back to normal." And with those few words, I realize how fragile my beginning had been and that if she had taken the advice of her friends, I wouldn't be here. And then my mind is filled with thoughts of my daughters. They wouldn't be here either—like a mass casualty event leading to the elimination of generations.

I look down at my lap and blink, not only to clear the black spots but to hold back the tears. My entire life, I never once considered that Jean might have thought about aborting me.

She takes a deep breath. “Well, obviously, I didn’t do it. I guess, more than anything, I didn’t feel I could do it to God,” Jean says in a voice quieter than it has been while she looks down at her hands folded in her lap. “So I told him. I told Frank everything, and I begged him to forgive me. I told him it meant nothing and that it would never happen again. It was awful, but he said we could try to make it work, and he would raise you as his own. But it didn’t work out. He couldn’t get over it. He just couldn’t forgive me. It crushed me, but I guess I don’t blame him.”

"We divorced, and it broke my heart for so many reasons, including that I knew I couldn’t keep you. I would not get any financial support from Frank, and I just couldn’t ask my mom to help. She had remarried and had a seven-year-old son who was a handful. I even hated having to take Tom to Mom's. So, I decided to place you for adoption. I convinced myself I was having another boy, which seemed to make it a little easier. But when you were born, and they said, ‘It’s a girl,’ I changed my mind and decided I would keep you."

What? The hair on my neck stands up. Can she see my goosebumps? I almost had a completely different life, a life without my mom and dad in it and, ultimately, a life without my daughters.

“But when your mom came in with gifts for me and Tom, I knew I couldn’t disappoint them. They had been so kind and were so happy. So I gave you away, and I've never forgiven myself."

Tears fill her eyes, and I reach for her hand and give her words of truth that I hope will make her feel better, "I really want you to know that you did the right thing. I have a wonderful life with amazing parents who love me very much. I love them with all my heart, and I've never wanted anything different."

I hope my words convince her that she made the right decision. I know I'll never tell her about my fear as a child that she might show up at my door to take me away. That will always remain my secret, but just as I think that, she says, "I did try to get you back, though."

My stomach cramps as she dips her finger into the cup and stirs my childhood nightmares. It hadn't just been a silly childhood fear. It had been a possible reality. The person taking me away had always been faceless back then, and it terrified me. So hearing Jean speak those words is like hearing that the boogeyman is real and has been hiding under your bed all along.

"You did?" I say calmly, though my throat seems to be closing up.

"Well, I married Danny's dad not long after you were born, and I thought I might be able to get you back. Unfortunately, when I called the attorney who handled the adoption, I found out I was too late. I'd missed the deadline for changing my mind."

I'm holding my breath as if I don't know how it all turned out. The black-and-white photo taken the day my adoption was final flashes in my memory, the smiling faces of my mom and dad with me. How do I respond to this, and what exactly is my face doing right now? I know I'm not smiling, but I can't even feel my face. I exhale slowly and hope it doesn't come out like a "whew."

"When you were eighteen, I actually came to your house to try to see you."

And the hits just keep on coming. "Really?" How am I still conscious?

"Seven years ago, I flew to Illinois to visit a guy I knew who lived not too far from where your mom and dad were going when they left California. I wasn't sure if they still lived at the same address, but I thought I'd see. I figured that since you were eighteen and technically an adult, it would be okay if I stopped by the house, and if you were there, I could meet you. So my friend drove me there, and we sat in the car in front of your house, but I couldn't get up the nerve to knock on the door. So we just sat there while I hoped to catch a glimpse of you. Were you still living in the same house you grew up in when you were eighteen?"

"I was," I pause. "I was married and pregnant with my first daughter, but we lived with my mom and dad. It's probably a good thing you didn't knock on the door, though, since I thought you were . . . since I didn't think you were alive."

"What do you mean?"

The waters have gotten really deep in the last thirty minutes. "Mom said she told you they were going to tell me you had died, and that's what they did. You don't remember her telling you that? She told me you probably died of a broken heart."

"No, I don't remember. Why would they tell you that?"

I feel my lava start to boil and rise up at what feels like a criticism of my parents. No, that's not strong enough. It feels like an attack on my parents, and I try not to let it show in my voice. "I'm sure the story was just a defense mechanism. You know, kind of a way to make sure you wouldn't come knocking on our door one day." Ouch. I didn't intend for it to come out that way. The silence is thick. "Well, it all worked out anyway, right?" I say, trying to infuse some oxygen back into the room.

"Yes," she says, "you're here, and that's all that matters." She stands up. "Would you like to see the rest of the house?" That's a good idea, a change in the atmosphere. This conversation has been exhausting, or maybe because it's now going on 11 p.m., and it's been a really long day.

She takes me on the tour, and when we come to her bedroom, I practically shout, "Oh, are you kidding me? I have those same curtains in my bedroom!" I know the matching eyeglass frames and curtains wouldn't be a big deal to most people, but the coincidences are stacking up.

"I don't believe you," she says, laughing

"No, really!"

Before the end of the night, I notice we are finishing each other's sentences. I've never experienced this before. I've heard the debates about nature vs. nurture, and I'm beginning to see the support for the nature argument play out in real time.

We sit in the dining room now, and I tell her a few stories from my childhood. I regret that I forgot to bring my baby book with me. She brings out a couple of photo albums with photos of my brothers growing up. I see them dressed in Halloween costumes, holding Easter baskets, and opening Christmas presents. They had a happy childhood, too, and, for some reason, that surprises me. What was I expecting? I think I might have pictured Tom's childhood like a scene from Oliver Twist, with him huddled over a bowl of gruel, wearing threadbare clothes, and pleading, "Please, sir, may I have some more?" Ridiculous.

As I've said before, my childhood was as perfect as anything I could ever have imagined, so I'm surprised when a feeling wells up from the center of my chest. What am I feeling as I survey the childhood of my brothers? Sadness? Hurt? No, none of those really describe it. I continue turning page after page as I picture myself standing between those two boys in the middle of all the fun they appear to be having. Suddenly I recognize what I'm feeling. It's jealousy. Why did she keep them and not keep me? I've heard the story and know the answer, but it doesn't stop that feeling from sitting in my chest like heartburn. I point to a photo of my brothers holding Easter baskets with giant grins on their faces when words I instantly regret escape my lips. "There was room for me right there."

A wave of heat washes over me as the words hang in the air with no place to escape. There's no sign that Jean has heard me, though I know she has. I change the subject quickly, flipping the page. "So when do you think you'll tell them about me?"

"I guess I'm a little afraid to tell them. I will, but I just worry what they'll think about me, about why I gave a baby away, and especially why I never told them they have a sister. What if they think I'm horrible?"

"They're not going to think that."

"I guess not, but I still don't know how to even bring it up, and I'm wondering how honest do I have to be? I cheated on Tom's dad. How do I tell them that?"

I've got nothing. So I say nothing.

It's now after midnight. We've been talking non-stop, and it's time for Mark and me to go. Hugging me at the end of the driveway, Jean says, "I'll call you tomorrow, and we can get together, okay?"

"I'd love that! We have a lot of time to make up for. Night, Mom."

"Mom." It feels wrong leaving my mouth, but there's no taking it back. Why did I say it? My mom who raised me is my mom, a title that feels sacred and reserved only for her.

No one else could ever be my mom, not even Jean. No matter how excited I am to have found her, I walk away from the house like I've just cheated on my mom somehow, and I wonder if I have to call Jean "mom" from now on. That sinking feeling that has become an unwelcome but faithful companion shows up screaming, "Traitor!" I'm so sorry, Mom.

Uncharted Waters

The next morning, I call Mom and Dad to tell them the news. I'm both excited and dread it just a little. As wonderful as they have been in supporting my efforts to find Jean, I can't help but think how much easier it would have been for them if she had remained a ghost. If I had returned home at the end of my search with nothing to show for it and with no further thoughts of being anyone but their daughter. The end. A part of me thinks Mom may have hoped for that. I don't feel that way about Dad, but I hadn't been looking for another father. Even more than sharing the news, I want to get it over with so I can show them it's no big deal. My primary goal is to convey how much I love them and that nothing has changed between us.

Mom answers the phone. "Hello?"

"Hi, Mom! How's everything there?"

"Everything's fine. How about there? How's the search going?"

"Well, I found her."

Silence, though just for a few seconds, "Well, good! How did it go?" Does she sound happy? I can't tell.

"It went well. Obviously, she was really surprised." I rush on without taking a breath. "I met Jean's mother, too. She lives with Jean in Phoenix. They are both very nice. I got to tell them what an amazing life I've had and how she made the best decision by giving me to you and Dad."

There. It's out. Jean and Mae are nice, but they will never replace my parents. Nothing is going to change our relationship. At least, that's what I hope I've conveyed.

Mom asks, "Did you meet Tommy?"

"Not yet. He goes by Tom now and lives in the Bahamas. I have another brother too. His name is Danny. He's a year and a half younger than me and lives out here near Jean. He's married and has two sons."

"Did you get to meet him?"

"No. Neither Tom nor Danny know about me, but Jean says she's going to tell them. That will be some surprise, huh? It'll be fun to meet them someday."

We continue to talk about what's going on back home. I talk with my girls, and everything seems right with the world.

"Okay, Mom, I'll see you Friday. I can't wait to get back home. I love you," and I mean every single word.

I anxiously await Jean's call telling me when we can get together. I know she's working, but I look forward to spending every minute I can with her before we have to go home. Mark, his sister, and I do a little sightseeing, but I make sure we're back at the house by 3:00. I don't know when Jean's workday ends, and I don't want to miss her call. Finally, around 4:30 in the afternoon, she calls and asks me what I've been up to. I tell her, and when I ask how her day was, she says, "Well, I took the day off, so I didn't do much. I was so tired. Were you tired too?"

I don't hear her question because my ears stopped working when she said she took the day off. She's been home all day and didn't call? We've wasted a whole day when we could have been together and getting to know each other. Why do I feel like I've been stood up by a date? The rejection complex that so often presides over my emotions is speaking loud and clear, "*See, you're not that important to her. She didn't even want to spend time with you today.*"

She fills the silence of my non-response, "You and Mark want to come over, and we can all go out to eat?"

"That would be nice." A perfectly trite response, I figure.

An hour later, Mark and I are walking through a restaurant parking lot, with Jean and Grandma walking side-by-side in front of us. I study them as we walk. Jean is almost six feet tall and perfectly fits the "statuesque" definition. Her gait is similar to mine, or is mine similar to hers? She's wearing a sleeveless dress with a pleated skirt. My eyes trace down her arms to her fingers, which are long and slender. My fingers are short and shaped more like Fred Flinstone's, undoubtedly a contribution from my birth father's gene pool. She doesn't have much in the hip department. Me? I've got that department covered. My eyes move to my grandmother walking beside her. Ah, yes, there are my hips. Thanks, Grandma.

We order from the menu, and I discover Jean doesn't like cheese—cheese is my middle name—and she doesn't like rice either. How can this be? Maybe she's not given my favorite foods a good try, but she won't take a single bite of my dinner full of delicious cheesiness, despite my coaxing. That could partially explain the difference in our hip sizes.

Back at Jean's house after dinner, we sit at the dining room table wearing our matching glasses, looking over my baby album, which I remembered to bring with me. She examines each photo slowly as if trying to absorb my childhood. It's easy for her to see I was loved.

"I missed so much," she says as she turns a page. "Can you leave your baby album with me so I can show it to the boys when I tell them about you?"

"Sure. Did you decide when you're going to do that?" I try not to sound too excited, but I'm encouraged by her request and still hope there's a chance I'll meet Danny and his family while I'm here.

"I haven't decided." She says, putting my hopes to bed.

"I understand," I say, nodding, which I hope camouflages my disappointment.

Grandma brings out more photo albums, and I hear her stories of days gone by, including how my ancestors moved from Oklahoma to Arizona, or “the Arizona Territory,” as Grandma calls it. I see photos and hear the names of aunts, uncles, and cousins, which all jumble together. I will undoubtedly forget the names before the day ends. Seeing the facial similarities, especially the eyebrows, which I’ve called my “golden arches” for years, is nothing short of fascinating. Many in the photos bear this prominent trait. Who gets excited about eyebrows? Me.

Grandma loves to talk and tell stories, but she also loves to listen. She’s easy to love. I learn that Jean’s brother Ronny, the uncle I spoke to just a day ago, is estranged from the family. They haven’t spoken in a few years. I’m told the story of what caused the estrangement between them. The issue is minor in the grand scheme of things, certainly not big enough to never speak again. Grandma’s pain as she shares the details is palpable. I can clearly see her sadness over losing a child who’s still alive.

I hear about Jean’s sister, who I’m told took her own life eight years earlier and who also placed a child, a baby boy, for adoption. I wonder where he is and if he has questions about his birth family. The scenario quickly plays out in my mind with him ending up here, only to find out his mother isn’t. How differently my story could have played out.

The next day, Jean and I go shopping. It’s the first time we’ve had a day together, just the two of us. While we’re walking around a department store, looking through the clothing racks, Jean suddenly grabs my arm and pulls me around a corner near the dressing rooms. Peeking around the corner, she looks panicked. "It's Danny's wife. Wait here," and off she goes.

I look around the corner and see Jean talking to my sister-in-law and young nephews while I wonder, "*Is she going to tell her? Maybe she'll tell her. No, she won't tell her before she tells Danny. Why are you hiding? She doesn't know who you are. This is ridiculous.*" Finally, gathering the courage to emerge from my hiding place, I wander a little closer to them while pretending to browse the clothing racks. Then, Jean is walking back towards me. "I'm sorry," she says. "Let's just wait here for a minute until they leave." I've never felt more like a secret and try to convince my face not to show it.

We spend the few remaining days of our visit doing much of the same. Mark spends time with his sister while Jean and I shop, have lunch, and then have dinner together. When our trip comes to an end, I'm a little sad. We still have a lot of time to make up for. I love Jean's stories, especially about her dating escapades, and I've never had anyone in my life laugh at the same things I do and say the same things I do at the exact same time. But it's time to go, and I am excited to get back to my daughters, my parents, and my life.

As we stand in Jean's family room saying our goodbyes, Grandma takes my hands and begins to pray, thanking God and asking Him for travel mercies for our trip. It takes me by surprise. Every prayer I've ever prayed with another person has been reserved for bedtime, holiday meals, or in a church building. I've never experienced someone praying like that, just out of the blue, standing in the middle of a family room. But it's nice. I like it. We stand, holding hands with heads bowed, and all join in the "Amen."

Jean drives us to the airport and walks us to the gate. As she hugs me, my tears aren't just about saying goodbye. They represent the end of a long journey that began fourteen years ago with my first glimpse of a black-and-white photo of the person who gave me life. All those years of wondering if she was still out there, of wrestling with doubt and uncertainty. It feels like a big wedding that was years in the making, brimming with anticipation and excitement, and now it's over. Or is it?

Where do we go from here? Is this the start of a beautiful new relationship, or will the initial thrill fade with time?

I have a family that I'm excited to get back to. How will my newfound family fit into that? It's like swimming in an ocean of uncharted waters. The only thing I know for certain is that God is in control.

My birth mother, me and Mom

Second First Birthday

After I've shared most of the stories of my trip with Mom and Dad, I remember one more thing, "Oh, Dad, I almost forgot! When I was at Superior High School, they had all the graduation photos from the last year hanging in the office. One girl had the last name Zacatenco, and I thought, I've only heard that name once before. That's your friend Tony's last name, isn't it? Is this how he spells it?" I ask, writing it down.

"Yep, that's it," Dad says.

"You should ask him if he has family there. There's probably only a one percent chance he's even heard of Superior, Arizona."

Dad laughs, agreeing with me. The following week, he shares this tidbit with Tony, and Tony's jaw nearly hits the floor. "I grew up in Superior, and my brother still lives there! What in the world was Amy doing in Superior?"

Dad then fills Tony in on the birth mother search story. Tony's curiosity is piqued, and he asks, "What's her birth mother's name?"

“Jean, and her maiden name was Hawkins.”

Tony’s eyes widen. “Was her husband named Frank Vazquez?”

“That’s right,” Dad confirms.

Tony’s face can’t hide his disbelief. “You won’t believe this —Frank was my best friend! We joined the Navy together, and I was the best man at their wedding!”

Seriously, you can't make this stuff up.

When Dad tells me the story, my eyes widen with every word. Is this a “what a small world” moment, another incredible coincidence, or another God thing on an ever-growing list of God things?

I call Jean to tell her the story about Tony and Dad, ending with, “Do you remember him?”

“I do! He was Frank’s best friend! That’s unbelievable!"

“I know. I can’t believe he was the best man at your wedding! What are the odds of that? Like a bazillion to one?”

I think we might spend a little more time marveling at it, but she quickly moves on to the next topic.

“I was going to call you. I told your brothers about you this afternoon. You know Tom’s here this week for a visit, so I called Danny and told him I needed to talk to him, and he said, ‘Okay, shoot.’ I said, ‘No, in person. Can you come over? I want to talk to you and your brother in person.’

"When he and Tom sat down with me at the kitchen table, I pushed your baby book across the table to them. They sat there looking at the cover, and both asked, 'What's that?'"

"And I told them, 'It's your sister.'"

"Then the words came pouring out as fast as I could tell them. When I finished, Danny said, 'Geez, Mom, we thought you or Grandma were dying or something!' And they both started laughing. It was hysterical."

Relief floods over me. I don't ask her if she told them the "whole" story, including the part about her affair. There's really no reason to go there, and I'll never mention it unless she does.

"They both said they're going to call you."

"I'm so excited and can't wait to talk to them!" Then I ask, "Hey, do you want to talk to your granddaughters?" I don't wait for an answer. "Hold on, let me get them."

Both girls spend a couple of minutes each talking to Jean for the very first time, and then I'm back on the line, and we wrap up our call. Later that day, Danny calls.

"Hey, sis! It's your brother, Danny. Welcome to the family!" He sounds a little southern, which I think is weird since he lives in Arizona, but then I recognize it as the same cowboy drawl that my uncle Ronny had. Danny is funny, and we laugh for the entire twenty minutes as we talk about our lives.

Tom calls that evening. "Hi, Amy, it's your brother, Tom."

"Tommy, that's what I've always called you, you know. I've known about you ever since I can remember." This call is more emotional for me.

"You have?"

"A photo of you taken when you were about two years old has sat on my dresser since I was eleven. You sound a lot older than I expected." We laugh. "Jean . . . I mean your mom . . . I mean, our mom gave my mom and dad a few photos to give to me." I realize what I call Jean will change depending on who I'm speaking to. It's going to get confusing. She's always "Jean" at home, but do I have to call her "Mom" to my brothers? I'm not sure.

We spend the next half hour laughing about his life in the Bahamas and how excited he is that I can finally "be around to take care of Mom." He laughs when he says it, but I don't think he's joking.

"Hey, why don't you come out to Arizona in February, and we'll have a birthday party for you? Introduce you to the rest of the family. What'dya say? I'll be back in Arizona then, and I'd love to meet you!" And that's exactly what we do.

My daughters and I fly to Arizona in February, and Jean and Grandma finally get to meet my girls. Meeting my brothers is extra special for me. I feel like I've known them forever. My brother Danny towers over me and everyone else, at 6'8". For the first time in my life, I'm the shortest person in the family.

My "first" birthday party includes food, music, and a big birthday cake with frosting spelling out, "Happy First Birthday, Amy," complete with a #1 candle. Jean's house fills with family and friends, including her on-again-off-again boyfriend. Our story fascinates everyone, and whenever I turn my head, I see someone staring at me. I know my resemblance to Jean is the reason, but I feel a little like a bug under a microscope. It's lovely and uncomfortable, exhilarating and exhausting, all at the same time. Like an actress in a play, I smile, talk, and laugh until the real me needs a break, and I end up in the guest room with the door shut, despite the promise I made to myself that I wouldn't run and hide.

This is my first time seeing Jean in a room full of people. She's quiet, and I see her introvert showing. It's evident to no one but me that I've received this gift from her. I can also see what Jean really loves about the man she's dating, who stands beside her. His larger-than-life personality is a yin to her yang. It's easy to see he has never met a stranger, and every word out of his mouth is a punchline. Jean doesn't have to say a word. She's happy to fade into the background when she's with him. I get it.

The party goes on until the wee hours of the morning, and while I truly appreciate the effort that went into it, I'm relieved when the last guest leaves, and I can finally stop smiling.

As our vacation draws to an end, I'm more than ready to go home. We've had a fun time, but this isn't home.

The week after we get home, I'm helping with a class party at my daughter's school when I overhear her talking about our trip to Arizona with another child. When he asks her, "Why doesn't your mom look like you?" Without hesitation, she replies quite matter-of-factly, "That's because my mom was adopted."

A Parade of Moments

A year after I find Jean, Mom decides to take a road trip to Las Vegas with one of her friends. “I thought we’d stop in Arizona and visit Jean,” she says without looking up from her crocheting to see my reaction, though I’m not sure my face reflects anything at all as I try to process what she’s said.

“Really? Well, that should be fun. You want me to call Jean and let her know?”

“No, I’ll call her later.” Mom brushes it off and is clearly done with this conversation as we move on to other topics.

When the day arrives for Mom's visit to Jean's house, I can't help but wish I could be a fly on the wall. I spend the day imagining their conversation and eagerly awaiting a call from Mom with a detailed play-by-play of the visit. But as the hours pass, the call never comes. With no way to reach Mom, I’m left to let my imagination run wild, picturing the most likely scenario: everyone gathered around the table, enjoying coffee and cookies while exchanging a few stories. That’s how I hope it goes, anyway.

A week later, when Mom finally returns from her trip, she calls, "I'm home!"

"Great! How was your trip? Did you have a nice time?"

"We did! Great weather, too."

Ok, enough small talk. "Did you get to see Jean?"

"Yes, we did. Had a nice visit."

"Grandma Mae sure is nice, isn't she?"

"Very nice."

We've said "nice" four times. Nice —Probably the laziest adjective in the English language. Adequate, acceptable, blah, blah, blah-de-blah.

The questions are clamoring in my head, begging me to let them out. "*What did you talk about? Did Jean ask about the bride doll? Did she ask why you told me she had died?*" But I push them all away and don't ask a single one. The discussion about their visit is over, never to be mentioned again. I don't ask Jean about it, either. Since Mom didn't seem to want to talk about it, asking Jean would feel like a betrayal of my relationship with Mom, like gossip somehow. Honestly, it just doesn't seem to matter anymore. Mom apparently got closure for whatever felt undone for her, and I have to assume Jean did, too.

Two years after finding Jean, she and Grandma come to visit us, and I get to show them the home I grew up in, where Mom and Dad still live. I don't mention that Jean has seen this house before, at least from the street, and I hope the topic doesn't come up. It might be hard for Mom to hear that

Jean had actually sat in front of our house, intending to meet me when I was eighteen.

Mom has made dinner, and we eat at the dining room table, which is always reserved for special occasions. After dinner, I give Jean and Grandma a tour of the house—the place where I learned to walk and where all my childhood memories were made. There's a surreal, almost dreamlike quality as Jean stands in my old bedroom, where I begged God to let no one come and take me away. The person I feared in those prayers never had a name or a face, but here she stands. The time and place of her reentry into my life perfectly orchestrated by God.

The following year, Jean and I take our first vacation together, flying to the Bahamas to visit Tom. As we board the plane, she says, "Please don't tell anyone I'm your mother." The words pierce my heart.

"Really? Why?" Surely I misheard her.

"I just don't want anyone to know I'm old enough to be your mother."

This is a new one for me, and I can't begin to comprehend it. Is it vanity? I don't know, but it feels like I'm being hidden again. All this time, I thought calling her "Mom" made her feel good, but it doesn't feel that way now.

"Well, alrighty then." Do I sound snarky? I feel snarky.

During one of my trips to Arizona, Jean asks if it would be okay with me if she goes on a date with her still on-again-off-again boyfriend while I stay home with Grandma. I assure her it's okay, but that's not true. I'm only in Arizona for six days, and she can't spend all of them with me? But, whatever.

That evening, I'm sitting with Grandma when she mentions her son came by that afternoon for a visit. Now, I know she hasn't spoken to Ronny in years, but more importantly, I've been here with her all afternoon. So what's happening?

"Oh, yeah? He came by today?" I ask, expecting her to correct her error.

"Yes, this afternoon."

I'm not exactly sure how to proceed. "So, how's he doing?" I ask, playing along.

"Oh, he's good. He just dropped by to say 'Hi.'"

Grandma's visitor is one of the first signs of the Alzheimer's disease that will lead to Jean eventually placing Grandma in a memory care facility where she will die in 1999, at the age of eighty-one. For the rest of her life, Jean will lament, "How could I put my mom away like that?" and nothing I or anyone else can say will lessen her guilt.

No matter how much time we spend together or how often we talk, Jean always feels more like a friend than a mother to me. When I visit her, we shop and go to movies and restaurants, and when she visits me, we shop and go to movies and restaurants. The only thing changing is the location. We enjoy being around each other, and our similarities go far beyond our appearance. We often compare notes on health issues and share many of the same.

Not long after Grandma dies, Jean is diagnosed with breast cancer. The prognosis is good; she's caught it in time, and I add one more item to the "History" section of my medical record and to that of my daughters. I know it's good to be aware, and it's what I've always told myself I wanted to know. Still, a part of me remembers with some fondness the ignorance-is-bliss state of mind that used to accompany the word *adopted* on my medical charts. I'm now answering some questions with checkmarks in the yes box. "Breast cancer?" Check. "Alzheimer's?" Check.

Déjà Vu

Jean and I, distanced by 1500 miles, have settled into a relaxed routine of occasional phone calls. Meanwhile, I'm fully immersed in raising my daughters, who are my everything. The term *helicopter mom* didn't exist then, but the term describes me perfectly. I pour my heart and soul into their activities—flute and piano lessons, voice coaching, ice skating, dance, gymnastics, band, orchestra, church plays, high school theater productions, and the list goes on.

I spend my days shuttling them wherever they need to go and making sure they practice everything they need to practice. I'm the room mother during their grade school years, and we attend church every Sunday. I sew costumes for every event, not just for my daughters but for any cast member who needs one. One year, I stitched giant vegetable costumes for a dozen high school students for a community service presentation and crafted elaborate costumes for the summer Shakespeare program, all in just a few weeks. After finishing the costumes, I'm in the auditorium for every rehearsal and performance, helping with ticket sales or whatever the director and his wife need. I chaperone every class trip, even though my daughters, once they're in high school, would rather I didn't. I know I might be a bit of an embarrassment at times, but it doesn't bother me. They are my world.

Discipline is never a problem. My daughters are respectful and are not rule breakers at home or anywhere else, as far as I know, and they are at the top of their classes academically. I feel blessed beyond measure.

When my oldest daughter asks to attend her first boy/girl party at a friend's house when she's in junior high school, she assures me the parents will be home. When I drop her off in front of the house, she's surprised when I turn off the car and get out.

"Where are you going?" she asks.

"To meet the parents," I say, and the look on her face tells me that probably won't be happening. We proceed to the door anyway and ring the bell. A boy opens it, and several other kids are inside, with music blaring. He looks from her to me and back at her.

"Hi, I just wanted to meet your parents," I tell him, smiling bigger than I want to.

"Oh, they went to get some sodas. They'll be right back."

"Okay, we'll wait in the car," I tell him, turning around and heading back to the car. We get in, and I turn on the radio.

About two minutes later, she says, “We can go.” And we do. Nothing else needs to be said. That’s about as far as discipline has to go.

All that being said, it’s no surprise to me when my marriage to Mark ends after fifteen years, though everyone we know is in shock. Our marriage has always been cordial and, by outward appearances, the perfect union, especially when we sat in church every Sunday. There were never any fireworks displays of anger. It’s all very civil and kind. So what happened?

My daughters have always come first and my marriage second, but it didn’t really seem to matter. Mark has been supportive and enjoyed their extracurricular activities, so he made that part easy. He required little of me. When my oldest entered her senior year in high school, Mark created spreadsheets ranking the universities she might attend, and we took cross-country trips touring the campuses. Two years later, we repeat the process with my youngest, and after we drop her off at college; I try to imagine my life as an empty nester. What kind of life do I have without them? Missing them while they’re away at college is soul-crushing, and I regularly struggle to hold back the tears.

Then one fateful fall afternoon, Mark and I go for a walk. We walk in silence as we usually do until I ask, “Would you like to go on a cruise?”

“I don’t think I’d enjoy that.” His answer, without a pause and so matter-of-fact, says more than the words themselves.

"But you would, wouldn't you?" He asks. They're not angry words. There is no accusatory tone in his response. He's made it clear before this that he's ready for retirement and not interested in new adventures. It's at this moment that my future flashes before my eyes. It's not the first time. I'm now thirty-seven, and he's turning sixty in a few weeks. Our twenty-two-year age gap, which didn't seem like a big deal in the beginning, has been getting noticeably wider, and his quick response is my first indication that he's noticed it too. Our marriage just seems to exist with no ups, no downs. We are two very nice and polite people living in a very nice and polite house, complete with a white picket fence.

"I think a cruise would be fun," I answer, thinking just for a second that maybe he'll give it another thought, though I know it won't be much fun if his heart's not in it. We continue to walk, and then he says out loud the words we've both been thinking, "I think we're done, aren't we." It's a statement. There's no question mark at the end.

But I answer anyway, "I think so." The words leave my mouth like the release of a breath I've been holding for a very long time. There are no tears. We walk silently as my mind spins with what this will look like.

"What's for dinner?" Yes, that's his next question. See? I told you, it's all very polite.

"Pot roast."

"That sounds good." We walk a little further in silence, and then he says, "I'll move out next weekend." And that's exactly what happens. We have pot roast, and he moves out the following weekend. The divorce is final just a few weeks later.

It's a strange feeling when a divorce comes out of apathy —when there's no fighting, no tears, and no harsh words. When everyone you know is stunned by its sudden demise and when they ask, "What happened?" you don't even know for sure what did. And then you realize it's more about what didn't.

I'm sad for him because he really is a nice guy and deserves someone to grow old with, and I'm sad for me because I don't know where I fit into a world where I'm single. I've been alive for thirty-seven years, and I've never lived alone before. I don't know where I go from here. Oddly, I'm never sad about the death of a marriage that has withered away. Like a swimming pool with a slow leak in the liner, one day, you notice the water is green and almost gone. You're not surprised because you haven't paid much attention to it for so long. You could repair it, but what's the point if no one wants to swim in it anymore? How many marriages end because of indifference? I'll bet the number is higher than anyone could ever think.

This divorce is a bigger shock to my system than my first one. I hate numbering my divorces even more than I hate numbering my marriages, by the way. Each divorce is an emblem of failure, a promise broken. After my last divorce, my girls and I lived with my parents. Now, with my daughters away at school, I'll be living in a house devoid of another human. At least I have my little dog. Then one week after Mark moves out, my dog dies, officially turning my life into a bad country western song. I fill the void by getting a Westie puppy I name "Merffy," who introduces himself by eating the baseboards in my kitchen and will become my faithful companion for the next sixteen years.

When The Dark Moves In

A few months after my divorce, *<cue the theme song from the Twilight Zone>* things start to happen that make me feel like there's more in that house than just Merf and me. Now, I don't want to go all "Beetlejuice" on you, but to this day, I don't have a scientific or even rational explanation for the events that took place at that old house.

The first incident happens at night, because don't they always? While I'm taking a bath in the second-floor bathroom, I hear the sound of something shattering coming from downstairs. Heart beating out of my chest, thinking someone is breaking in, I climb out of the tub, throw on my robe, and run, dripping, down the stairs without even a broom to defend myself with (an instinctively stupid move on my part, much like every soon-to-be-dead character in a scary movie).

Entering the living room, I find an 8 x 10 framed photo of my oldest daughter lying broken on the floor about four feet in front of the living room fireplace. For over a year, this photo has been sitting on the back of the fireplace mantel with several 5 x 7 framed photos in front of it. Those smaller photos are still sitting undisturbed on the mantle. I stand there, barely breathing, looking from the mantel to the mess on the floor while trying to figure out how this large photo fell so far away from the fireplace like it had been thrown and without disturbing the ones standing in front of it. I can't muster a logical explanation and jump to the fairly ridiculous possibility that this is some sort of omen and that something has happened to my daughter, who is attending college over 1,100 miles away and is living in the dorms at school. This is before mobile phones, and I try in vain to reach her via her dorm hall phone as my worry escalates with each passing hour. Would anyone notice if she hadn't shown up to class?

My imagination takes over with all the horrific possibilities, and needless to say, I don't sleep at all that night. The following day, when I can no longer wait to speak with her, I call the dean's office and leave a message explaining that it's urgent that I speak with my daughter. Three hours later, receive the call, "Hello, Amy. This is Dean Whittaker, and I have your daughter here for you. One moment."

"Mom? What's wrong?" Her voice is frantic.

"I'm so relieved to hear your voice. Are you okay?" I can barely speak as the relief leaks from my eyes.

"I'm fine. Is everything alright? What's going on?"

Dare I tell her? "Well, I was taking a bath last night when I heard this crash, and I came downstairs to find your photo, you know, the one that sits on the mantel? Anyway, it was broken on the floor, and the photos in front of it were still sitting up there and how did it fall without hitting the ones in front of it? I don't know. And it fell like four feet away from the fireplace, like it leapt off the mantel."

She interrupts, "Mom . . . "

But I'm on a roll, "When I couldn't reach you on the dorm phone . . . "

"Mom. Mom. I'm fine. I don't understand what you're saying."

"I thought it was some kind of omen or something. I don't know."

"Really, Mom?" Clearly, she thinks I've lost my mind.

"I know I sound crazy, but it just didn't make any sense." I pause at the silence on the other end of the line, "You must think I've lost it."

"Well, maybe a little. I'm fine, though. I'll call you later, K?"

"Okay. I love you."

"I love you too, Mom."

Hanging up, I realize I sounded insane and can't imagine what she told the dean about the reason for the call. Could it all be an overactive imagination in this silent house? Thinking it was an omen? Yes. But the mysterious leaping photo? No. I didn't imagine that.

As days pass, I will continue to hear noises coming from upstairs when I'm downstairs and from downstairs when I'm upstairs—nothing loud like a crash, but random sounds that are loud enough to get my attention. I keep telling myself that I'm simply not accustomed to living alone and that these are the sounds an old house makes. Settling, that's it. The house is settling.

Then, one evening (because, well, you know, the dark and all), I'm sitting in the recliner in the living room, crocheting and watching *American Idol* on TV, when Merf, who is lying on the couch, suddenly sits up. His eyes start darting along the ceiling like he's tracking a fly, except it's winter, and there are no flies. He jumps off the couch and runs to the foot of the stairs in the foyer. I can only see halfway up the staircase from where I'm sitting, frozen mid-stitch, as I watch him panting and furiously wagging his tail at whatever has his attention on the second floor.

Then I hear it, *thump, thump, thump, thump,* as his tennis ball comes bouncing down the stairs into view. He grabs it, holds it in his mouth, and continues looking up the stairs with his tail still wagging. I still haven't moved and may not even be breathing for all I know as I strain to listen for footsteps upstairs over the sounds of *American Idol*. I turn down the TV but don't turn it off because I'm not sure what would be worse, silence or the sound of something actually moving around up there. Merf finally loses interest in whatever captured his attention and returns to the living room, drops his ball in front of me, and sits down, waiting expectantly to continue this impromptu game of fetch.

"What'd you see, Merf?" I ask, finding my voice. If he answers me, I'm getting in the car.

"Nothing to see here," I keep telling my fully creeped-out brain. But maybe that's the problem. It definitely feels like something is there, whether I can see it or not. It takes me a minute to muster up the courage to put down my crocheting and walk over to the stairs. Merf picks up his ball and follows me. His tail is wagging; mine is not. I look up the stairs, where I see nothing but the dark. Unlike any horror movie I've ever seen, I actually turn on the stairway lights and stand still, listening for any sound from the floor above. You know, the sounds of the house settling. When all I hear is the TV, I start up the stairs with Merf bounding ahead of me. I wait three stairs from the top to see if he runs into a particular room, but he stops at the top and looks down at me. Is he smiling?

"Go get 'em, Merf," I say. But he just stands there looking at me like he's wondering what I'm doing. "What am I doing?" I ask myself. "Do you really think someone is hiding in your house just so they can throw pictures from the mantel and play with your dog?" What exactly am I looking for? Ghosts? I examine every room and closet, and yes, even under the beds, confirming there's no one here but Merf and me. Right? Someone, please tell me I'm right.

The broken picture frame and bouncing ball incidents have now awakened a fear of the unexpected at home, especially at night, and bring back memories of the ghost from my childhood. He wore a bowler hat, lived in my closet, and only came out at night when the wind blew, waking me in terror. But that well-dressed ghost stopped visiting when Dad put a chair against the closet door to keep it from rattling.

Things go missing from time to time, never to be seen again. Dog toys, my grandson's teething ring, and random objects of little importance just disappear, but the truly creepy stuff seems to have calmed over the last couple of weeks.

Then, one morning before work, while sitting at the dining room table eating a bowl of cereal, I hear something small hit the floor in the kitchen behind me. I look over my shoulder and watch a quarter rolling toward me until it stops at my feet. I pick it up and examine it. It's a silver quarter dated 1959, the year I was born. Coincidence? Perhaps, but where did it come from, and why did it fall on the floor all by itself? I know there was no coin lying around my kitchen and I add it to the list of unexplained events now happening even in the daylight.

My next-door neighbor, who is seventy-two years old, grew up in my house. In fact, her father, Henry, built it in 1940. When I tell her the story about the quarter and the other events, she's convinced it's the ghost of her father, who she tells me was a coin collector and died in the house just a few years before we bought it. Good to know, or maybe not.

I've never been a believer in the dearly departed haunting the living. I believe in heaven and hell, so how do I reconcile the idea of a spirit hanging around to interact with the living after its body dies, like it missed the bus to wherever it was supposed to go? Regardless, I yell, "Henry, I'm home!" when I get home from work every day.

I haven't had another of these weird, unexplainable occurrences in a couple of months, but as I wait for the next one, something else comes over me. It creeps in slowly. Maybe giving a name to whatever it is in this house (if there is an "it") and yelling a greeting to it every day may have been a bad idea.

"Don't be silly," I tell myself. But it feels far from silly. It feels dark and definitely not good. There's this feeling that is so subtle. You know what it feels like when you can feel someone staring at you? And then you turn around and see that someone IS staring at you? It's like that. Only when I turn around, there's nothing there.

I don't share this weirdness with anyone because I know how crazy it sounds, especially to me, the most rational person I know.

Living alone helps me clearly see how my entire life has revolved around my daughters, and in living only for them, I lost myself. What purpose do I have without them?

To escape the emptiness, I throw myself into the dating pool. It doesn't take long to see that the pool is polluted and filled with more frogs than princes. After ending one particularly toxic relationship with one of these frogs (who I'll not-so-affectionately refer to as "Froggy"), I look at myself and once again think, *How did I get here?* The only control I seem to have is what I eat, or more precisely, what I don't eat. I've lost so much weight that I look like a walking skeleton. I haul my miserable self over to Mom and Dad's apartment and lie on their couch because my house feels like it's filled with sadness and because I secretly believe I may be starving to death. You don't realize how much of yourself you've lost until your eighty-seven-year-old mother is begging you to drink a can of her Ensure.

Emptiness fills me. Is it depression? Is it loneliness? I think about Jean's sister, who took her own life. Is this genetic? I don't know. I've been sad before, but never anything like this. But then again, I've never been this alone and purposeless before.

With curtains drawn, I sit on the sofa in my living room, holding a bottle of pills. Sad music plays on the stereo because despair is always better with a soundtrack. The hopelessness I've been feeling has turned into something much darker, and what started as whispers in my head are now yelling and drowning out every other thought. "*You're not much good to anyone, you know. No one really needs you. It would be easy to stop the pain and not be lonely anymore. It would be easy to end it."*

I've always thought suicide was a horrible, selfish act. How can it now feel like the best option I have?

Admit it. It doesn't feel that crazy now, does it?

Now I'm arguing with the voices, "Stop it. Just stop it. It would hurt my girls. It would hurt my parents." What is happening? Am I losing my mind?

"*Really? Then why are you holding those pills? Don't worry; they'll get over it. Really. They'll all get over it.*"

Where are these thoughts coming from? I've never felt so empty of everything good. I press my hands against my ears to shut out the voices, but they're not coming through my ears. It's like a battle between good and evil, and it's not only in my head—it's swirling in the air around me.

"God—please help me." The words escape my lips in a voice that doesn't even sound like my own, a moan through my sobs. I'm surprised by the words because I haven't thought about God in a very long time, but they're the only words that come, "God, please help me," over and over—an SOS prayer to the extreme.

That's when the doorbell rings, Merf barks and everything seems to stop moving, though I can't explain exactly what was moving. *I'll just sit here, and whoever it is will go away.* The doorbell rings again, so I go to the window and peek through the curtains. I see a flower delivery truck parked out front, and a man holding a floral arrangement stands at the front door. Who would send me flowers? Maybe they're from Froggy, who has realized he can't live without me. My heart fills with hope despite knowing that letting him back into my life would be insanity.

Flower Guy must see the curtains move because he rings the bell again and knocks on the door for good measure, sending Merf into a bigger frenzy. Wiping my face with my shirt, I go to the door and catch a glimpse of myself in the foyer mirror. I'm a mess. There's no way to improve what Flower Guy will see, and for probably the first time in my life, I don't care what I look like. I open the door just enough for Flower Guy to reach through and hand me the flowers. "I'm very sorry," he says, apparently thinking someone must have died based on the condition of my face.

"Thanks," I grunt, taking the flowers without eye contact and shutting the door as quickly as possible. Setting the flowers down on the dining room table, my pulse races in anticipation of what's sure to be a love note from Froggy. I open the card, and my spirit sinks. "Happy Easter, Love, Mark." See, I told you my ex-husband is a nice guy.

What kind of oblivious haze have I been in to forget tomorrow is Easter? I shudder at the thought of how close I came to—I can't even say it. What a tragic and sickening Easter memory that would have been for my parents and my daughters. I shake my head like an Etch-a-sketch trying to erase the visual and turn off the stereo that's now playing "Alone Again Naturally." Shut up, Gilbert O'Sullivan. I open the curtains to let in the light, wash my face, put on my tennis shoes, and set off on a walk with Merf.

We walk for three hours while I think about the horrible irony of the words I'd heard in my head. The exact words Jean's friends had said to her when she found out she was pregnant with me almost forty years ago. The words that hurt so much when I heard her say them, "It would be easier to end it." They meant the same then as they did today, the end of me. The definition of abort is to bring about a premature end. I wonder why they don't call suicide an abortion because, in essence, that's what it is: a premature ending of a life. It's clear to me now that "*It would be easier to end it*" are words straight from the devil, who wants nothing more than to terminate the gift of life God has given us. There's a reason Jesus calls Satan "the enemy."

When I return home from my walk, the shadows have lengthened, and streetlights have come on. The darkness, depression, or whatever had wrapped around me like a burial shroud is gone. What has changed? Why does everything feel so different now? Could this be God's answer to my desperate prayer, 'God, please help me"?

The Dreaded Day

Mom is eighty-seven when she falls and breaks her hip. Actually, reverse that. She was just standing there when her hip broke and she fell. They can't repair it, so she will never walk again. Dad and I learn how to help her get from her wheelchair to any other seated place using a belt to lift her. She's only five feet tall and all of ninety pounds, so it isn't heavy lifting. My heart breaks as I watch her fade away.

During this time, an X-ray shows a large spot on her lung. She's not a candidate for a biopsy, but the doctors say it's almost certainly cancer, which is no surprise since she's been a smoker for over sixty years. They offer no treatment plan, and we're told to call hospice so we can keep her comfortable. A hospital bed is delivered to the middle of their small apartment living room. Dad is a wonderful caregiver, and my sister, nieces, and I relieve him as much as possible, sitting with Mom, spending the night on the couch next to her bed, and giving her pain medication. A single tear rolls out of her eye as a farewell to her dignity when we change her diapers.

The morphine helps with the pain but leads to hallucinations.

"Mac, get that cobweb down," she says to Dad.

"What cobweb, Teeny?"

"That one," she says, pointing to the ceiling over the patio door.

There's no cobweb, but Dad gets the duster and climbs on the step stool to brush the imaginary cobweb away.

"Did I get it?"

"There's another one," she says, pointing to another spot.

Dad never complains. He just keeps clearing away Mom's cobwebs with a smile, a little song, or one of his infamous sayings that he's repeated so often that everyone can say them along with him.

The week before Mom dies, she tells me, "You make sure your dad goes for his bone scan on Wednesday."

"I will, Mom."

Between Mom's broken hip and the mass discovered on her lung, and maybe because bad things do seem to happen in threes, an annual doctor visit determines that Dad's prostate cancer has returned. He's been in remission for five years since his radiation treatments, and his scheduled bone scan will determine if the cancer has spread.

"I'll be there, Teeny. Don'tcha know, don'tcha know, don'tcha know," Dad sings in one of his classic responses.

"Tell your dad he's got to get some new sayings," Mom says to me in all seriousness, but we all laugh.

The following day, Mom's pain seems to be worse. She's barely conscious and moaning, "Ho hum. Ho hum." Over and over again. The same "Ho hum" her mother chanted forty-one years ago when the car accident claimed her life. I call hospice again and they increase her morphine. The moaning ebbs, and now she's still, unmoving, silent except for her breathing, which you can hear if you lean close enough. Her mouth is dry, and when I try to moisten her tongue with water, little pieces of her tongue fall off and stick to the sponge.

It's January 31, 2001, and a winter snowstorm is raging. The wind howls as if it's making the noise I long to make but can't. I have to maintain composure for Dad, who is putting on his coat, hat, and boots, to leave for his bone scan.

"I'll be right back, Teeny," Dad says, kissing Mom on the cheek. I watch him drive away into the blizzard. I wish I could have gone with him, but I have to stay. If it's Mom's time to go home, I must be with her.

"Please keep him safe, Lord," I pray, pressing my eyes to keep the tears from falling. I sit down next to Mom and take her hand. Suddenly, she opens her eyes, which have been closed for two days. I look into those crystal blue eyes that I've looked into all my life. I think she sees me, but I can't be sure. "I love you, Mom. You're the best mom anyone could ever have." There's no sign she's heard me, and her eyes close again. It will be the last time I'll ever see them.

My sister, niece, cousin, and I wait while watching Mom's chest rise and fall. It's irregular now. I hate the small talk we fill the air with. I can't bear to see her suffer like this anymore. We are to watch her feet for mottling, a sign that the end is imminent. I dread lifting the blankets to check, and when I do, I see the purple spots, the awful harbinger of death. I call the hospice nurse again.

"Mom's feet are mottling, and her breathing is really irregular."

"I'll be right over. Would you like me to call the chaplain?"

"Yes, please."

The nurse arrives within the hour, and the chaplain arrives soon after. It's been three hours since Dad left. I keep going to the patio door, hoping and praying I'll see his car pull up. The snowstorm is still howling. The chaplain prays with us as we form a circle around Mom's bed. Then she says, "Tena, I hear you like bingo. Is that right?"

Mom, who hasn't responded to anyone in the last two days, replies with a breathy "Uh-huh." I gasp out loud.

"Well, I hear they're holding the bingo game for you in heaven," the chaplain continues, "and it's okay for you to go. Everyone here is going to be all right."

"*NO! WAIT!*" my brain screams, *"DON'T GO, MOM! Please wait till Dad gets home!"* But the words stay inside my head.

Minutes later, Mom takes one deep breath and ever so slowly exhales. She's gone.

I've never known a world without her in it, and it feels like my heart has just broken into a million pieces. I know, I know, time will heal, but the Mom piece of my heart that belonged only to her will always be missing. I know that as I sit on the bed next to her, holding her hand, which stays warm for a very long time. I remove her wedding band and put it on my finger, where it will stay until my daughter removes it from my hand someday. Mom's color is fading to gray and her jaw drops open like Marley's ghost in "A Christmas Carol." I don't want Dad to see her like this when he gets home. Why is it taking him so long?

I ask the hospice nurse, who is also waiting for Dad's return, "Is there something we can do so Mom will look better when Dad gets here?" All I can think of is the handkerchief that was tied around Marley's head to keep his jaw shut.

The nurse gently closes Mom's mouth. "Can you bring me her teeth?" Mom's teeth have been sitting in a container filled with water for more than two weeks. I get them, and the nurse puts them in. "How about some blush and lipstick?"

I'm not sure if we want to go full-on beauty queen here. "Okay, maybe a little blush. No lipstick, though." I really don't want her to look like she's ready for a night on the town.

When Dad's car pulls up, I go to the lobby to meet him and wrap my arms around him. "She's gone, Daddy."

"I was afraid of that," he says, removing his black fuzzy snowcap. Brushing the snow off it, he holds it to his chest like he always does with his hat when a flag passes by as a sign of honor and respect.

Entering the apartment, he walks up to Mom's bed and lays his hand on her arm. "We had forty-five wonderful years, didn't we, Teeny?" After patting her hand, he walks to the bedroom they once shared and sits on the side of their bed. I follow and sit down beside him.

"Are you okay, Daddy?"

"I'm fine, li'l sweetheart," he says, patting my knee. "We've been saying goodbye for a long time, haven't we?"

"We have, but that doesn't make it any easier."

"No, I reckon it doesn't."

After the coroner leaves, two men from Science Care arrive. Years ago, Mom and Dad had made arrangements to donate their bodies to science when they die, and as they prepare to take Mom, I return to the bedroom where Dad is watching Woody Woodpecker cartoons on the TV.

"Daddy, they're here to take Mom. Do you want to say goodbye?"

"No, honey, we said all our goodbyes."

I can't bear to watch them cover her head, so I stay in the bedroom with Dad, my heart heavy with each muffled sound coming from the other room. When the apartment door finally closes behind them, I return to the living room. All that remains of her is the faint impression on her bed, a stark symbol of her absence. I sit down beside it, running my hands over the spot that still holds a trace of her warmth. Lifting her pillow to my face, I breathe in her scent, letting grief consume me as I sob into the pillow, desperate to keep my cries silent so Dad won't hear. When I finally gain control of myself, I go back to Dad and sit next to him on the bed again.

"What are we going to do without her, Dad?" The tears start falling again. I can't hold them back.

"We'll be okay, li'l sweetheart," he says, putting his arm around me.

"What about you, Dad?" The thought of him living alone is more than I can bear.

"Oh, I don't know. Maybe I'll move down to the Old Sailor's Home in Mississippi."

There's no way I'm letting him leave me. "I thought that maybe you'd like to come live with me. What do you think?"

"Oh, I couldn't do that. You're a young, single lady, and I don't want to cramp your style." He ends that statement with a giggle.

"I don't have a style, Daddy. I'd love it if you'd come live with me."

"I'd like that," he says, patting my hand and smiling. It's settled, and I've never been more certain about a decision.

We pack his bag and I take him home with me. It will be him and me against the world from now on.

When Frogs Scream

Remember Froggy? Well, he's back, and I'm still letting him create havoc with this on-again-off-again relationship that has gone on (and off) for almost two years. Might as well tattoo "Certified Idiot" on my forehead.

About a month after Dad moves in with me, I finally come to my senses over pancakes with Froggy at a local diner on a cold and gloomy Saturday in March.

"Where do you see our relationship going?" I blurt it out because you know when the end is the end, and I no longer care what he thinks.

Froggy looks at me like I just asked him to calculate the square root of an armadillo, and then he says, "I can't tell you what I'm doing tomorrow, let alone in the future."

"Well, I can tell you what I'm doing tomorrow and the day after that, and it doesn't include you. So please take me home."

We leave the restaurant and drive the three miles back to my house in complete silence. When I get out of his truck, he doesn't even wait for me to close the door before he's squealing tires as he tires out of my driveway. This time, I have no tears, no burning in the pit of my stomach. Instead, the oppressive weight I've been carrying throughout this wretched union lifts from me as I walk into my house. Even the sound of his screeching tires is like a symphony of my freedom.

I walk into the living room, where Dad sits in his recliner, watching TV. "Hey, Dad, would you ever want to move away from here, away from the snow?" I already know the answer. Dad and I have talked for years about leaving the Midwest winters for lands of warmth and sunshine, but Mom would never leave.

"Sure! Where do you want to go?" he asks, turning down the TV.

"I was thinking Arizona. What do you think?"

"That sounds good. When do you want to go?

"Yesterday," I reply as I walk upstairs to get Jean's phone number.

I've always been a bit impulsive, but this tops the list. Not once do I think about the job market in Arizona or leaving behind everyone and everything I've ever known in the place I've called home my entire life. But no matter, I call my realtor to let him know I want to list my home in the spring once the snow melts and everything is in bloom. He comes over the next day to give me an idea of market value, and just a few days later, he calls to tell me he's got a buyer willing to pay above market value if I sell it to them now. Well, I guess we're selling now, then.

I'm thrown into a bit of turmoil after accepting the offer. I book a flight to Arizona and spend a week there finding a home for Dad and me. I'm excited about living near Jean and getting to know her and my extended family better. I think my brother, Tom, is happiest of all since he has moved back to Arizona and has always felt his role is looking after Jean. He now sees me as helping with that task. The home-buying experience also inspires me to get my real estate license once I get to Arizona. The future feels bright, but I'm a little unnerved about how fast this is all going, and waves of "*What am I doing*?" wash over me daily. I know the move to Arizona will be great for Dad, who loves to golf and also represents a new beginning for me. But am I running away? Maybe. After the death of my mom, two failed marriages, and a horrible relationship that almost destroyed me. Who wouldn't want to run away? I feel like a strong and independent woman with this decision.

The following week, I'm sitting in my car, during my lunch break, lost in a book, when there's a knock on my window. Startled, I look up. You've got to be kidding me. It's Froggy. I get out of the car, taking a deep breath, and that's when he sweeps me into his arms (yes, I let him) and asks me to marry him.

Can a person choke on air? My mind and my heart spin. This is the commitment from him I had dreamed of. The commitment I had thought would fix everything. It doesn't matter that I've sold my house and have a home in escrow in Arizona. It doesn't matter that I'm training my replacement at work or that Dad has already given his car away to my niece. More importantly, it doesn't seem to matter that I know this relationship was forged in the fires of hell. Still, here I am, actually contemplating marrying this man, who has been a constant source of misery. Women, I ask you, why do we do this? Surely I'm not alone. Maybe it's a genetic quirk or something that dates back to Eve and the snake.

With my heart pounding, I tell him I'll think about it while my brain is screaming and beating on my skull: "*SAY NO! SAY NO! SAY NO!*"

I can't focus for the rest of the day at work, and that evening, when I get home from work, I tell Dad about this latest situation. "Hey, Dad, he asked me to marry him." He knows who I'm talking about. There's only been one, and Dad has watched this circus from the front row.

Dad's face changes. My happy little daddy looks sad, and it's not a look I've seen him wear very often. "I think that would be the biggest mistake you've ever made." And this is significant because Dad has never offered me relationship advice. Never. Not once. Boyfriends, two marriages, two divorces, and not one word of advice. He would have if I'd ever asked, but I never did. However, he's seen how this relationship has eroded his little girl, and I know he's afraid of what will happen if I say yes.

I spend the next two days contemplating my options, as if I really had options. Then the answer becomes apparent. When I think about marrying Froggy, I see dark storm clouds. Well, I don't actually *see* them, but I feel them. It smells, too, like the ozone in a lightning storm. When I think about moving to Arizona, I feel a lightness of being and hope. Like sunshine, rainbows, and unicorns, if unicorns came with a feeling. When I tell Froggy I can't marry him and that I'm leaving, he makes a sound like I've never heard coming out of a human being, and it's more than a little terrifying. Like a guttural howl from a dying creature, perfectly capturing the moment of my release from whatever held me captive.

Dating the Devil's Stand-in

Dad and I begin our life in Arizona and it's everything I could have dreamed of. I'm studying for my real estate exam, and Dad's prostate cancer hasn't spread and treatment is going well after eighty-eight radioactive isotopes are placed in his prostate. But then, complications set in, which result in a permanent urostomy (a tube coming out of his abdomen from his bladder). The doctor appointments are many, and Dad's journey is quite painful, but he handles it all as he always does, with humor, smiles, and repeating the same sayings Mom had suggested he retire. It's not exactly the sunshine, rainbows, and unicorns I'd predicted, but it's close.

After getting my real estate license, I'm juggling seven-day workweeks with caring for Dad. When Jean suggests I start dating, I think, "How on earth would I find time for that?" But eventually, I dive into the wild world of online dating, which, let me tell you, is not for the faint of heart or those with a low tolerance for the world of weird.

I go on a few of these blind dates, including one memorable evening where the guy takes off his shoes and asks me to rub his feet after dinner. I'm thinking, "Whoa, buddy, foot rubs are like VIP privileges reserved for at least date number four." But that's just my rulebook. After only three of these online escapades, I decide I'd rather spend evenings watching TV with my dog and delete my profile from the dating website.

Then, just days later, a man strikes up a conversation with me while I sit in the waiting room during Dad's urology appointment.

"Don't worry, a vasectomy isn't as bad as it sounds," he says. "Your husband will be fine. I just had one and was surprised at how little pain I had. The incision . . ."

I interrupt him so he'll say no more of what already feels like too much information. "I'm here with my dad, and he's definitely not getting a vasectomy."

We laugh over that bit of awkwardness, and after we chat for a bit, he writes his name and phone number on a piece of paper and hands it to me.

"You're not married?" I ask, somewhat confused.

"Nope, never been married."

"But you just had a vasectomy."

"Yep. Don't want kids either." That should have been my "run like the wind" moment, but no.

When I tell a friend about this guy, she asks me if I've "Googled" him. What in the world is a google? Nothing shows up when she walks me through it, which I guess means he's not made the news as a serial killer, so I decide to give him a call.

After a few dates, it's obvious to me that we're far from ideally suited, but I figure at least he makes me laugh and doesn't ask me to rub his feet. It's a low bar. We end up dating for almost a year. Then, one day, while we're watching a parade, a float from a Christian school passes by, and he says, "I'd like to put all Christians on a boat and set it on fire," while laughing like it's the funniest thing anyone's ever said. You know that statement, "Your blood runs cold?" Well, I now know personally what that means, and I stifle my urge to punch him in the throat.

"So that's what you want to do to me? Put me on a boat and set me on fire?" I ask in all seriousness, and he laughs even harder until he realizes it's not a punchline, and I'm not laughing.

"You're a Christian?" he asks, eyes widening as if I've just revealed I'm an extraterrestrial. What have I ever done to make him think I'm not a Christian? I'm such a good person. Look at how nice I am and all the good things I do. But then I think, *what have I done to make him think that I AM a Christian?* And that's when my spirit crumples. We've been together almost a year, and he doesn't have a clue that I love Jesus. If he can't tell, can anyone? Maybe I need to punch myself in the throat.

"Yes, I'm a Christian."

"Really?" Long pause. "Wow."

"Why do you think that's a bad thing, being a Christian? Set us on fire?"

"Where do I start?" is all he says, his face twisting in disgust.

"Just take me home," I reply, wondering if my face looks as disgusted as his. We don't speak at all on the way home as Jimmy Buffett sings "Cheeseburger in Paradise" on the radio. I feel like I'm riding with the devil and can't wait to get out of his car.

This relationship is over, but it's just the beginning of something else. I want to find a church—no, I *need* to find a church.

What? No Organ?

I've shared my faith journey up to this point. You'll recall that I was raised in church and baptized when I was ten. I answered an altar call from Billy Graham at twelve and even wrote Jesus on my shoes in a feeble attempt to spread the gospel.

Church Amy has sat in the pew with her Bible in her lap and her tithes in the collection plate. Church Amy has sung in the choir and taught pre-schoolers in Sunday school. Church Amy has made sure her daughters went to Sunday school and Vacation Bible School and made their costumes for every church play, rehearsing their lines and all the songs they sang. She taught them to pray before bed and the holiday meal, just like she'd been taught to do. Yes, Church Amy was a good person who did all those good churchy things, but outside the church building, she didn't give Jesus a thought, and her Bible collected dust. I also realize that everything I attribute to Church Amy is in the past tense. I haven't set foot in a church in a few years. What's a few? Oh, maybe ten years would be my guess.

When I move to Arizona, I spend any free Sunday I have hiking in the mountains alone. "I feel closer to God up on that mountain than I do in any church building," I tell anyone who asks me where I go to church.

Jean attends church every Sunday and asks me to go from time to time. Jean also watches televangelists on TV every day, which I don't understand. The way they constantly ask people to send money feels wrong, and the fact that Jean sends them some of it disappoints me. I feel like they've put one over on her. Can't she see who they are with their big hair and pinky rings? I tell you this so you'll know why I never wanted to go to church with her. If this is her style of preaching, count me out. But since my "burn the boats" incident, I'm on a mission to find a church, and she's thrilled when I ask to go with her.

We arrive at the church Jean attends, which is about forty-five minutes from my house. I doubt I would ever drive this far for church regularly, especially living where there's practically a church on every corner.

I'm shocked at how massive the church building is. Walking through the parking lot, it's immediately clear to me that I'm overdressed, and the few women wearing dresses aren't wearing pantyhose <*insert gasp here*>. I see plenty of blue jeans, shorts, and even halter tops <*and another gasp here*>. Is this church in the twenty-first century? Have all churches gone casual while I've been away, or is this just an Arizona thing?

Entering what can only be described as a stadium with a stage, I guide Jean to the back, away from her usual seat near the middle. I explain, "Back here feels more comfortable to me." She doesn't seem to know anyone in this place, and I understand. She doesn't have to speak to anyone and feels she can easily disappear in a church of this size. The music starts. I look around me for a hymnal, but there are none. Instead, the song lyrics are projected on giant screens around the auditorium. I don't recognize the songs, and I'm not sure how I'm supposed to sing along if I can't see the music score.

There's no choir, just a group of people on stage with microphones and a full-on band! Guitars, keyboards, and, wait for it, drums! Yes, drums! Where's the organ? How can you have church music without an organ? The music is loud and fast, nothing like the traditional hymns I know by heart. No "Onward Christian Soldiers," no "Old Rugged Cross." The songs are simple and repetitive. If you can handle "Row, Row, Row Your Boat," you're good to go. There's no story in the words that sound more like a chant to me. Regardless, everyone seems to be getting into it. Soon, smoke is billowing, and lights are flashing. It's all so theatrical that I expect the pastor to come down out of the ceiling, sitting on a disco ball or something. What kind of rock and roll church is this? I watch in awe as hundreds clap their hands, dance in the aisles, and raise their hands to the ceiling. Standing beside me, Jean raises her hands, and I feel a flush of embarrassment rise on my cheeks. Surely, I don't have to do *that*. I have never raised my hands or clapped along with the music in church, not ever, and I don't intend to start now. Apparently, I am the "frozen chosen" personified. In fact, every muscle is tensed as I stand there, mortified, in my church dress and pantyhose. I'm slightly damp under my arms even though I can practically see my breath with the air conditioning that's apparently set to "Arctic Tundra." I sing the words on the screen under my breath while I watch the show around me and feel less at home than I've ever felt.

At the close of the service, we all bow our heads as the pastor prays. At the end of his prayer, he instructs us to keep our heads bowed as he calls out, "Raise your hand if you need Jesus!" I raise my hand because who doesn't need Jesus, right? With my head bowed, I hear Jean whisper, "Do you want me to go with you?"

My eyes pop open, and I drop my hand and look at her. "Go with me where?" I see a man coming towards me as other men lead people to the front of the church. I feel like I've been tricked by the church version of bait and switch. Panicking, I shake my head "no" and wave my hand to dismiss the man before he can reach me and embarrass us both. I whisper back to Jean, "No. No. I didn't know. I don't want to go up there." I can't wait to get out of here and know I'll never return. If you asked me an hour later what the sermon was about, I couldn't even tell you.

Uncomfortable as it was, the experience doesn't diminish my quest to find a church. Over the next several months, I try on several and, just like Goldilocks, I rank them: this one is too small, this one is too big, the music is too loud, too rowdy, too lifeless. As far as the preaching goes, I figure if I fall asleep during the sermon, this is not my church. I visit so many churches but don't feel like God is in any of them, and this is what I tell Jean, who often accompanies me on my Smorgasbord of Churches Tour. Then one day, she tells me she thinks she's found a church I might like. And she's right. I love everything about this church, the music, the pastor, and, most of all, it feels like God is here. We start attending together regularly, but "busy, busy, busy" often gets in my way. The weekends, you know, are busy real estate days.

Battle of Wills

When I meet TJ, another agent at my office, one of the things that attracts me to him, over and above his dashing good looks and charming personality, is that he actually goes to church. This means I don't have to worry about him putting me on a boat and setting me on fire, which has now apparently moved to the top of my list of qualifications in a mate. When we start dating, we attend church together, and not long after; he moves in with me and Dad because Dad and I are a package deal, as every guy I have ever dated has been informed.

Living together without marriage is something I've never tried before. But, hey, it's the twenty-first century, and everyone seems to be embracing the "try before you buy" mindset. I've always been more of a "don't serve up the milk unless he's bought the cow" kind of person, so this arrangement feels light-years outside my comfort zone. I tell myself that not wanting to get married again makes this the best choice for us both, but honestly, I don't really buy it.

For the record, the saying, *love is blind,* is really a thing. It doesn't take long for TJ and I to recognize how different we are, especially after moving in together. *Well-matched* is not a phrase anyone would have used to describe us. *Incompatible* is probably more like it. But we bind and gag that word and shove it in the closet, only pulling it out when we can work it into an argument.

Jean knows everything that's happening in my relationship with TJ. She's been my dating confidant from the beginning. I share every happy moment and every disagreement. I love that she understands because she's been there, empathy in the flesh. But when she tells me, "God doesn't want you having a sexual relationship with someone outside of marriage, so He's not going to bless this relationship. It will always be a struggle to live that way." I can hardly contain my annoyance. She lived this exact same way until just a few years ago, and it feels like a great big box of hypocrisy wrapped up in a self-righteous bow.

It should have made me examine myself, but it only makes me examine her. Seated beside her at church one Sunday, the communion tray passes by as soft music plays, and the lights are dimmed. When I take the tiny cracker and a tiny cup of grape juice, Jean leans over and whispers, "People who take communion when they're intentionally sinning can get sick and die."

That familiar volcano stirs inside me. I can actually feel the lava bubbling. "Don't be silly," I whisper back, while deep down wondering if what she says is true. I quickly toss the cracker in my mouth and chug back the teaspoon of juice without a prayer, without a moment of thankfulness, with no reverence whatsoever. A demonstration of defiance that has nothing to do with "This do in remembrance of Me." My head is bowed, but I'm not praying like everyone around me. I have no thoughts of the suffering and sacrifice Christ made for me. No, instead, I'm brooding about how hard it is to have my own personal Judge Judy sitting beside me. Poor me.

When TJ and I can be at church together, we are. It's like something we check off our Sunday to-do list. Sometimes, our feelings are stirred when one message or song resonates more than another, but that's all it really is: a feel-good moment that we leave right there in the pew when we exit the building.

Two strong-willed people living in the same house cannot do so happily without concessions that neither of us is willing to make. Our disagreements turn into arguments and soon become the norm. I'm no longer the little girl running away from confrontation. I've found my voice, and I'm not afraid to use it to defend myself and retaliate whenever I feel wronged. I also develop a powerful skill to accompany my voice called "the silent treatment." Harsh words and silent treatments, the perfect one-two punch. TJ, by the way, already holds a black belt in those two techniques. We step into the ring like street fighters, wearing blinders but no other protection, skillfully throwing that one-two punch to prove our points and win. But there are no winners. We both end up emotionally bruised and battered. Those blinders, though, work perfectly to keep us from seeing anything but the fight, and they certainly keep us from seeing how God would want us to handle things.

This battle of wills chips away at our relationship, and one day, the tree will fall. I'm sure of it. But until then, we remain together even though love shouldn't feel like this. We've been down this road before with five divorces between us, my two and his three. There's no honor for either of us in those numbers that only confirm the odds are stacked against our relationship surviving.

By all outward appearances, our life is good, at least by the world's standards. I'm very successful in business, and even though my relationship with TJ is more turbulent than any relationship should be, we have plenty of good moments, too. I'm living the American dream, going to church regularly and tithing, too. I'd pat myself on the back if my arms were just a little longer.

When Jean reminds me again that my relationship with TJ is volatile because we're living in sin, I laugh and think, "*How very archaic. Living with someone outside of marriage isn't a big deal to God. He's a God of love, so as long as you're in a loving relationship, it's all good. Anyway, the world changes, right? We can't be expected to live exactly like the Bible says we should, can we? I mean, it was written thousands of years ago. Things are different now, right? Right? Hello?*" Is that an echo?

There's no defining moment when worry overtakes me. It comes on slowly. Fear, plain and simple: the fear of living without: without my father, whose health is declining; without money and all it provides if I don't work hard enough; without love, as my relationship with TJ crumbles. Living without these things scares me. Living without Jesus should have scared me more.

But Now I See

There is no earthly way for me to explain what happens on Sunday, June 27, 2004. When I get out of bed, it's no different from any other Sunday, and TJ and I sit towards the back of the church, as we always do. The pastor is giving his testimony of how he came to faith in Christ, a testimony I've heard before. But towards the end of his story, something happens. In an instant, the room goes completely dark, and no one is there but the pastor and me. He's standing inches from my face and speaking to me alone when he looks into my eyes and asks, "Are you living your life according to the Word of God or are you distorting the Word of God to fit your life?"

The words are like a physical blow that penetrates my being. I'm trembling, and my legs grow weak as every lie I've been telling myself is exposed. I clearly see that I've lost my way, and there's only one way back. I can't keep living the way I've been living. My life has to change, and I can't do it without Jesus. Then it's suddenly light again, and I'm back in the here and now, and people are leaving the sanctuary. I don't know how long I've been "gone." Seconds? Minutes? TJ takes my hand. "Are you okay?" I nod, wiping the tears from my face. How can I explain what just happened when I don't understand it myself? I'm dizzy and still trembling as I try to process what feels like a literal come to Jesus moment.

We're only ten feet outside the building when I finally find my voice. "You have to move out. We can't keep living together. It's not right. It's not what God wants. We both know it."

Just like that. WHAM. Maybe I should have eased into it, but I really don't feel like I have control of anything at this moment.

TJ doesn't say a word, which is response enough to tell me he's not happy about my proclamation. When we get in the car, I try to explain what I just experienced and finish with, "This isn't about getting married. If you were to ask me to marry you right now, I'd say no. I don't want to end our relationship, but we need to start living the way God wants us to live. We need to each start our walks with Jesus, together but separately."

Again, there's no response, and we ride the rest of the way home in silence. I get it. I've just pulled the rug out from under him. There was nothing subtle about it.

As we approach the house, he finally speaks, "I'm going to my mom's."

I nod, exit the car, and watch as he drives away. This may be the end of our relationship, but for the first time, I'm not afraid of losing him. There's no doubt in my mind that this is the path we, or at the very least I, need to take. I'd love for TJ to join me, but I won't change my mind if he doesn't want to.

I spend the next three hours thinking about how long and how far off the track I'd wandered. Honestly, I'm not even sure I knew there was a track, but it's all crystal clear now. Oh, I had Jesus in my life. He was always "right over there." I loved Him, but I didn't know Him. I'd wave to Him from a distance as I rushed around on a quest to find that one thing that would complete me; the perfect relationship, more money, more success, shiny objects, or the next best thing to make me look or feel like the next best thing. You know, all the things the world tells us we need to be happy, but never satisfy. All I can hear in my head right now is, "*I was blind, but now I see.*"

When TJ returns home a few hours later, he's changed. I don't know what happened to him while he was gone. That's between him and God, but I believe God worked a miracle in him as much as He did me. It's decided. TJ will get an apartment nearby, and we'll be faithful to God. We'll also be faithful to each other in sickness, health, and what feels almost impossible: in chastity.

The next day, we meet with our pastor to ask him for guidance as we share our decision to walk with the Lord. We tell him we've made a lot of mistakes in our lives, but one of our biggest is not being a good example to our four daughters, who are now adults. He prays with us and connects us with a Sunday school class for new believers, as well as a women's group and a men's group for each of us. I've always believed in Jesus, so being tagged a new believer feels a little off, but then I realize there's a difference between believing with your head and believing with your heart. TJ and I agree that we both have so much to learn.

When you binge Jesus, it's life-altering. We see His presence everywhere. Instead of just stopping by church on Sunday to recharge our Jesus battery, we stayed plugged in. Dusting off our Bibles, we actually spend time reading and studying God's word every day. We can't get enough. It truly is a new life, and with it comes a change in our social circle. Some of our friends evaporate. There one day, gone the next. It's really quite remarkable, but it's okay. Our walk has changed, and we can't make them accept that fact. We're never going back to where we were.

We've come to another profound realization: the ultimate self-help book we ever needed has been sitting on our shelf all along, the Bible. It's truly awe-inspiring to realize that we can connect with the Author of that Book (and the Author of the entire universe, for that matter) at any time, day or night.

My prayer life changes, or maybe I should say it begins, since I never talked to the Lord regularly. Except for those SOS prayers cried out in desperation, prayer was a formal ritual reserved for holiday meals and church services.

Prayers were to be said using King James' words like "thee," "thou," and "thine." I approached God like Dorothy meeting the Wizard—minus the giant green head and flames—feeling more than a little intimidated and entirely unqualified. But now, my prayers are like having a heartfelt conversation with a loving father who genuinely cares and understands me.

A few months after we give our hearts to the Lord, TJ asks me to marry him, and a December 18 wedding is planned. We also reaffirm our commitment to Christ by being baptized for the second time. TJ was baptized as an infant in the Catholic church, and I, as you'll recall, at ten. But this time, it isn't about something you do (or is done to you) at a certain age. This time, it truly signifies our rebirth in Christ. I should add that Jean is thrilled to learn of our newfound faith and that we are no longer "living in sin."

During service one Sunday, I have a thought that comes out of nowhere: *"You should let the youth pastor know you paint children's murals."* I haven't painted a mural since I moved to Arizona and haven't given it a single thought during that time. So, I'm surprised when it comes out of nowhere. *Do I really want to paint a mural? When will I have time for that?* Yes, that's me arguing with the voice in my head. The voice wins, and I leave a note the following morning for the youth pastor, letting her know I would be happy to volunteer to paint murals in the children's building should they want any. The next day, I receive a call from the youth pastor who tells me she and her assistant were out of the office the day I left the note. They were touring churches to get ideas for the children's building and both decided murals would be incredible, but it wasn't in the budget. Only to return to the office to find my note. So, I now spend most of my free time painting murals in the children's building at church. Every room has a different theme: Noah's Ark, Jonah and the Fish, Moses parting the Red Sea, David and a two-story Goliath, and the list goes on. I pray that God guides my hand with each mural, and He does. Each completed project is a work of art far beyond anything I could have imagined. I also have to tell you that every single mural I paint coincides with a crisis in my family and not just little things; I'm talking big things, life-threatening things, tragic things. Between these painting projects, everything is calm, and life goes on as usual, but as soon as I start another mural - Shazam - all hell breaks loose, literally, and I begin to wonder. Is the devil mad and trying to keep me from painting? Perhaps. But I don't stop. I keep praying, and I keep painting.

When I begin a mural depicting Jesus and the children in the main hallway, it's the first time I've ever painted an image representing Christ. Then, as if the devil gets the memo, calamity strikes. But, this time, it's a double whammy that will truly be a test of our faith.

Round 1 - Return to Sender

For months, Jean has been telling me she's lonely. We spend hours together when she helps me with those murals at church, and it's there that I hear of her loneliness the most. I offer suggestions like participating in some of the many events at the retirement community where she lives or volunteering at church, the hospital, or the library. But she tells me she doesn't really like socializing and doesn't want a schedule to keep.

I have always been a fixer, and I'll be the first to admit that I have little patience for anyone who continuously complains about a situation but makes no attempt to fix it, so my patience is growing thin. When the pastor's message on Sunday is about loneliness, it feels like a gift from God, at least to me. It's an uplifting message about God's presence and is full of remedies for loneliness. I sit quietly beside her, wrapped in vindication, while my brain yells, "*Can you hear that? He's saying exactly what I've been telling you!*"

The message concludes with the story of a lonely woman who offered her time to the Lord, and soon, her loneliness was nothing but a memory. There it is. I'm entirely justified. Surely, she sees herself in the story of the lonely woman and will finally stop complaining and do something about it. She says nothing about the message over lunch after church. Instead, she brings up her loneliness again. Did she not even hear the message this morning? When I tell TJ how frustrated I am with it all, he says, "You're complaining about it as much as she is. Either talk to her about it or stop complaining about it." Good point.

So the following day, I wrangle up the courage to speak to her about it and call her while driving to an appointment. *For future reference—never, ever, EVER ask anyone what they thought of Sunday's message if you think it applies to them.*

After our general "What's new?" conversation, I ask, "So what did you think of the message at church yesterday?"

"What do you mean?"

The tone in her voice is all but shouting and waving its arms, "Danger! Abort! Abort!" But do I heed that warning? No. Instead, I continue, "The stuff about loneliness."

"Yeah, what about it?"

This is not going to go well, and hindsight being 20/20 and all, I should have just left it right there and changed the subject, but I plod ahead, "I was just thinking about your loneliness and what the pastor said about giving some time to the Lord. Do you think . . . "

And just like that, her head explodes. "Who are you now, the Holy Spirit? I was saved when I was ten years old. I don't need you to save me."

Wow. Save her? Really, all I want to do is help her fix her loneliness. My mind can't process what she just said or what I should do now. She's never spoken to me in this way, with a level of hostility I would never expect from her. My heart is racing, and I've broken out in a sweat.

"Okay, well, I have to go. Talk to you later," I say, snapping my flip phone shut and throwing it onto the passenger seat like it's on fire. I'm not angry, well maybe a little, but even more than that, I'm hurt, and my rejection complex erects a wall in record time. I guess she's angry and hurt, too, because she doesn't call back, and neither do I. What happens a few hours later, though, feels so much worse.

We rarely email each other, so I'm surprised when I see an email from her sitting in my inbox without a subject line. I open it and read the first sentence, "*I have stuffed my feelings around you for years.*" Wow, for years. All this time, I thought we had a good relationship. I was wrong. Following that proclamation is a list of all the things she doesn't like about me. Before I can even read the entire list of my flaws, I panic and click the delete button. I stare at the trash folder with my heart pounding, wondering if I should try to read the whole email. I can't. I click "Empty trash," and it's gone.

I sit at my desk, trembling. Conflict resolution is not one of my skills. Never has been. If I can run away from it, I will. I've become a master wall builder. It's always been easier to build a wall to hide behind than negotiate a peace treaty. The last thing I want to do is call her and give her another opportunity to shoot arrows at my heart. I don't want to hear her list of complaints about me spoken out loud. *My mom would never have done something like this,* I think as I sit staring at the screen. That much is true, and a fresh wave of missing Mom floods my heart. It confirms to me what I've thought all along, that Jean and I have never been more than friends. My eyes wander to the calendar on the wall, and it hits me. It's October 4th, twenty years to the day since I walked back into Jean's life, and here we are. Again, I think about God's timing. Was this in His plan all along? Twenty years. That's all. It's over. We will now return to regular programming. He can't be happy about what's happening, but what should I do now? I figure we'll paint the mural together the following day and sit beside each other at church next Sunday. In other words, ignore the whole thing. I'd be okay with that, sort of. I mean, I'm wounded, but surely it will scab over. Will it leave a scar? Probably.

But Jean doesn't show up to paint the next day or any day that week. She doesn't come to church on Sunday and will never walk through those church doors again. Just like that, she completely disappears from my life and my daughters' lives, too. Poof! She's gone. And to add insult to injury, my brothers go with her. My hurt over the whole thing turns to anger and will eventually become resentment. And like all resentment, unresolved, it turns into bitterness. <*Cue the sad violins*> I did nothing to deserve her treatment of me. Okay, I never called her either. Not when she didn't show up to paint and not when she stopped showing up at church. But, whatever. It was I who went to all that trouble to find her. It was I who moved across the country to be near her, and this is all I have to show for it: a list of the reasons she doesn't love me. I wear righteous victimhood like a cloak whenever I think about her. She didn't want me then; she doesn't want me now. *Rejected! Unwanted! Abandoned!* All the words I thought I had exterminated rise from the ashes and course through my veins. They were only hiding in the shadows, after all.

My birth mother has just stamped "Return to sender" on my heart. It might have been better if I'd never found her at all.

The bell rings, signaling the end of the devil's Round One. I may be wounded, but I'm still at church every day painting that mural. So, he goes for a knockout in the next round, which begins just a few days later.

So pull up a chair and grab a beverage for Round Two. It's not going to be pretty.

Round 2 - There Will be Blood

It's a routine colonoscopy. TJ has one every five years because of the colon cancer that runs in his family. The report is excellent, with no issues. Three days later, he's running a fever, and in so much pain he can't stand up. I call the doctor's office and leave a message. I don't get a call back for hours, but when I do, I'm told that even though he has five of the symptoms on the list of possible colonoscopy complications, it has nothing to do with the procedure.

Two hours later, TJ collapses, and I call 911. He's transported to the emergency room and admitted for what they believe is a bowel obstruction. This possible diagnosis makes little sense to me, considering his colonoscopy just three days prior. I tell them I think his colon is perforated. No one listens. We learn that the doctor who performed TJ's colonoscopy does not have privileges at this hospital. I'm unsure if this is a good or bad thing since I'm convinced he's the reason we're here.

It begins ~ We have no idea what lies ahead

The ER doctor inserts a nasal gastric (NG) tube, and TJ is admitted to the medical wing. I ask for a cot so I can stay overnight in his room.

The following day, TJ complains of constant pain and burning in his chest. I'm worried about the placement of the NG tube since the drain canister has remained dry. Don't we always have gastric fluid in our stomachs? Shouldn't there be something in the canister? When I ask his nurse about this, she asks me if I'm a nurse. When I tell her I'm not but that it seems logical that there should be some gastric fluid in the canister if the tube is working properly, she tells me I don't know what I'm talking about and walks out of the room in a huff. So I go to the Nursing Director, who comes to the room and determines the tube was indeed improperly placed and is curled up inside TJ's esophagus. An hour later, the NG tube has been replaced and so has his nurse, at my request. This will be the first in what will become a long list of medical errors that will forever change my view of the medical system. As with any profession, I suppose some are exceptional at what they do, and others are, let's just say, not so exceptional. But I will no longer assume the former.

TJ has been in the hospital for three days, and I'm now worried that his diabetes is not being properly managed. He's been a Type 1 diabetic since he was seventeen and has been on an insulin pump for several years. Since the day he was admitted, he's not been allowed to eat, and his blood sugars are not being monitored. Why is it taking so long to figure out what's causing his pain and fever? A couple of scans have been done, but we've been told nothing except that he may have a bowel obstruction. So why is nothing being done? Why is he just lying here and seemingly getting worse by the minute? Maybe it's because we're in the room furthest from the nursing station and next to the emergency exit, but I feel like he's been forgotten.

Today is day four of our hospital stay. I say "our" because I have not left the hospital since we got here, and I'm watching his whole body become pale. The pain medication keeps him pretty sedated, but when it wears off, he's groaning in pain. He looks thinner. How much weight can a person lose in four days? We have also been informed that none of TJ's doctors have privileges at this hospital, so I ask his attending physician if he will authorize TJ's transfer to the hospital across town so his doctors can treat him. He assures me TJ is getting the best care and doesn't need to be transferred. What we're actually experiencing runs contrary to that opinion.

In the meantime, it's been two weeks since that "situation" with Jean. For fourteen days, we haven't spoken. I think about calling her to let her know what's happening, but I know she receives the daily prayer chain emails from our church, and we've been taking up a lot of space on those prayer chains lately. And because I know she knows, her silence hurts even more. I just don't have the energy to deal with it right now.

A tech enters TJ's room to place a PICC line (Peripherally Inserted Central Catheter). I'm not allowed to stay in the room for the procedure, so I stand outside the door and watch as his bed is elevated as high as it will go. The tech cuts into his arm, then, looking like he forgot something, leaves the room with unconscious TJ lying there with no bedrails in place and bleeding onto the sheets. I'm confused as I watch the tech walk down the hall and onto the elevator. I stand at the door, poised to run into the room to catch TJ if he moves. The tech returns ten minutes later and completes the procedure.

TJ has still not regained consciousness, so I decide to go home for the first time since we got here. I'll shower and make sure Dad has everything he needs since he doesn't have a car. He's pretty self-sufficient and a pro with a microwave, and our wonderful friends have been bringing him home-cooked meals, which is greatly appreciated. Two hours later, I return to the hospital with my laptop, and my Bible.

TJ and I are full-time real estate agents, and the world has not stopped turning, contrary to how it feels in this place. Our clients are still depending on us, so working on my laptop and phone fills many of the hours I sit by his bed. I'm starting to believe this hospital stay may take longer than we thought. When I'm not working or hovering over TJ, I spend time reading my Bible and praying. There's nothing more I can do. We need God's help.

One of the pastors from our church comes to visit and prays with me while TJ sleeps. He doesn't like how TJ looks any more than I do, so he calls his son, David, an ER doctor at another hospital, who also happens to be our Sunday school teacher, to come to the hospital to see TJ. When David arrives, he walks around TJ's bed and checks the bags and tubes, then suggests we go to the cafeteria to talk. He says, "Now I'm talking to you as a friend and not as TJ's doctor, but a first-year medical student could tell you that TJ is in trouble. I advise you to call every doctor he's ever had. Be calm when you speak with them but let them know exactly what's happening and your. Put the risk of doing nothing in their hands and ask that he be transferred to a hospital where they can treat him. If nothing is done, I'm afraid pneumonia is going to be the next hurdle."

Just as he says those words, TJ's daughter walks up to our table. "The nurse just came in and said Dad has pneumonia," she says. We return to his room immediately, and while we walk, I tell David, “God can’t take TJ now. He just got baptized and everything.”

Then David says, “Oh, yes, He can." And with those words, I can’t hold back the tears. He continues, “We can be thankful for what Christ has done in TJ. If he’s called home, we know where he’s going.” These aren’t the words of comfort I had hoped for. I don’t want TJ in heaven yet. I want him here—with me. He finishes with, “But we will not give up. We’re going to keep praying for TJ’s full healing and trusting in the Lord.”

We pray together, and I struggle to say the words, “Lord, Your will be done.” I can’t bear the thought that God’s will would be to take TJ. What I don’t know at this moment is that this visit by David is just the first sign that God is right here with us and His will IS being done.

A couple hours after leaving messages with several of TJ’s doctors, he’s transferred to the hospital across town and admitted to the ICU, where he’s diagnosed with sepsis, an infected PICC line, pneumonia, and a perforated colon from a routine colonoscopy. The battle for his life will also include a pulmonary embolism (PE), Methicillin-Resistant Staphylococcus Aureus (MRSA), and countless other infections with names I’ve never heard of.

Ten bags hang on two IV poles and are flowing into his body. He has nine doctors, including Internal Medicine, Cardiologists, Endocrinologists, Infectious Disease

Specialists, and Gastroenterologists, to name a few. He's placed on a morphine pump and can have nothing by mouth, no food, no water, nothing except for an occasional small spoonful of ice chips.

Although the plan is to resect the colon to remove the damaged part, it's currently not possible because of the infection. Until then, the colon must be kept as dry as possible, so he's fed intravenously with a milky liquid called Total Parenteral Nutrition (TPN) through the newly placed PICC line. By the grace of God, the puncture in the colon has encapsulated, forming a kind of barrier that is keeping the toxins from leaking into his body, and that is buying him some time.

His diabetes makes everything more challenging, of course. Low sugar, high sugar. It's a daily rollercoaster as I try to play quarterback with the doctors, who often contradict each other with their specific treatment plans. Each night, I sleep on a cot in his room, never leaving his side except to go home to shower and check on Dad every four to five days, depending on TJ's condition that day. I always return to the hospital as quickly as I can, as I fear that while I'm gone, one of the many errors I've witnessed may kill him. This hospital is better than the last, but mistakes are still being made. I return more than once to find him sitting up and eating a tray of food, despite the "Nothing by Mouth" sign taped to his door. The miscommunications are unbelievable to me. I have always had such a high regard for the medical system, and that regard has now been shaken. When I return to TJ's room for a second time to find him eating, I yank the tray away as he yells at me for taking food away from a "starving man." —Good times.

Time in prayer and reading my Bible are my lifeline. I read the words written in red out loud and play praise music, hoping TJ can hear it even when he's unconscious. I can't count the number of times that I pick up my Bible, and at that very moment, someone from church walks in to visit and pray with us, like God saying, "I'm right here."

Prayers are answered when they finally find a specialist who can insert a drain through TJ's lower back and into the encapsulation surrounding the colon puncture, allowing the infection to drain. Until now, no specialist has been willing to try this because of the extreme risk of further injury and possibly causing a leak of the toxic fluids, which could kill him. It's risky, but I'm told it's our only option. He's not getting better. I pray so much for TJ's healing that I hope God doesn't tire of my nagging. When the drain is successfully in place, protruding from TJ's lower back and into a small bag, I thank God again. The drainage tube does what it is intended to do, but it's painful. The tube is stitched to his skin and pulls whenever he moves, sits, lies, and, well, pretty much all the time. The site becomes puffy and infected, but the tube remains. It often gets clogged with blood and secretions, and I'm shown how to massage the tube to remove the clogs. No matter how carefully that's done, the pulling on those infected stitches is always painful. To make it more comfortable, I fashion a thick pad out of gauze and tape it around the site where the tube comes out of his back, changing it four times a day.

When the doctors diagnose a pulmonary embolism, they put TJ on blood thinners, but they can't seem to regulate his blood clotting factor (INR) rate, which means he's at a high risk for blood clots. Why is this happening? I think about the TPN that's being pumped into his body as his only source of nutrition. I know it's mixed to include vitamins, minerals, insulin for his diabetes, and much more. Knowing how easily I bruise due to a vitamin K deficiency, I ask the nurse, "Is there vitamin K in that TPN?" She confirms that there is, and once they adjust the vitamin K, his INR levels finally stabilize. I ask why something so simple hasn't been thought of, but no one can or will provide me with an answer. Instead, I'm asked about my medical background, as many of my questions and theories are remarkably on point. I assure them I have no medical training and can only attribute my insight to God's guidance. Even as our confidence in the medical system wavers, our trust in Him remains unshaken. The doctors may provide medical care, but God is our ultimate source of hope and strength. He's the one we cling to.

Despite the initial hope that came with the insertion of the drainage tube, fevers and infections persist. The doctors, having exhausted all possible treatment options, say those awful words no one wants to hear: "We've done all we can do."

A few nights later, I'm confused when two orderlies arrive late in the day to move TJ to a different ICU room without notice or reason. In a rush, I gather my belongings and follow them as they push TJ's bed and IV poles down the hall and into the elevator. I've never been to this part of the hospital before. It's old, this original part of the building, like we've stepped back in time.

We enter his "new" room, and my heart sinks. The room is tiny and dark in more ways than one. It feels like a space that all hope has been drained out of. I know. I've felt this darkness before. Has TJ been moved here because there's nothing more they can do? He's been unconscious for two days. Is this where they take people to die?

"Why are you moving him here?" I ask, knowing they'd never admit that this is heaven's waiting room. All hope can't be gone. I refuse to accept that. I'm told they needed his other room for another patient and, "Oh, by the way, you can't stay overnight here because there's no room for a cot."

So maybe it's me, and they're just tired of me hanging around? Yes, that's where I go with it—stupid time for my rejection complex to kick in. I respond to his new nurse as sweetly as I can. I can't let him throw me out of here.

"I'm sorry, but I really can't leave. I'll just sleep here in this chair. Would you be able to bring me a pillow?" He is very kind and returns with a pillow and a blanket, but it soon becomes apparent sleep isn't going to come while sitting in a straight-backed chair, bent over a pillow on my lap. So I sit up all night, staring at the lights on all the machines.

I'm exhausted, but I try to pray. The only prayer that comes to mind is the 23rd Psalm: "*Yea, though I walk through the valley of the shadow of death, I will fear no evil: for Thou art with me; Thy rod and Thy staff, they comfort me."* It feels fitting, so I repeat it over and over. Just as I begin to drift off, TJ suddenly sits up with a sharp gasp as if he's struggling for air. My heart races as I leap to his side, my pulse skyrocketing from calm to frantic in an instant. He's panicking and staring up at the ceiling, clearly terrified. I try to calm him. "It's okay. They just moved us to a different room. I'm right here."

"Look! Do you see them?" His eyes are tracking something I cannot see.

"What, baby? Do I see what?"

"Them!" he says, pointing at the ceiling. "They're fighting for me. Look!" Then he falls back on the bed and is unconscious again.

I check to make sure he's still breathing and then look up at the room's ceiling, hoping this in-between world he witnessed will open up to me. I see nothing but ceiling tiles and shadows.

"Keep fighting for him," I whisper. "Please, keep fighting."

The next morning, I hate this ICU room even more than I did the night before. Even in the daylight, this room is dark. So I start my campaign to get TJ moved back to the other ICU wing. I walk through the hallways of that wing several times a day, hoping to find an empty room they can move him into. The next day, I find not just one but two empty ICU rooms, and I make my formal request to have TJ moved. Within hours, he's moved back to a room with light coming through the window and a cot for me—the squeaky-wheel theory in action.

TJ has been without sunshine on his skin or fresh air in his lungs for almost four weeks. So on a day when he's more alert than he's been in a while, I decide to take him outside for some fresh air and a change of scenery. I duct tape his two IV poles to a wheelchair, and we head to the elevator.

What a sight we are, and it's an adventure I'll only attempt this once. Getting into the elevator with all those wheels is more than a challenge, and I'm thankful for the helpful bystanders. Sitting outside the front entrance in the sunshine, I can see just how thin and pale TJ has become. I'm looking at his sunken cheeks and the dark circles around his eyes when I see him tear up.

"You okay?" I ask. A pretty silly question under the circumstances.

"Do they realize how blessed they are?" he asks, barely above a whisper, as he watches everyone coming and going. "Just to be able to get out of bed in the morning, to go to the bathroom by yourself, and to make a cup of coffee? I'll never take that for granted again."

I nod. I won't either.

"I'd sure love a burger right now," he says, gazing at a man carrying a McDonald's sack into the hospital. Then he says, "I'm ready to go back in now." What I thought might make him feel better has failed.

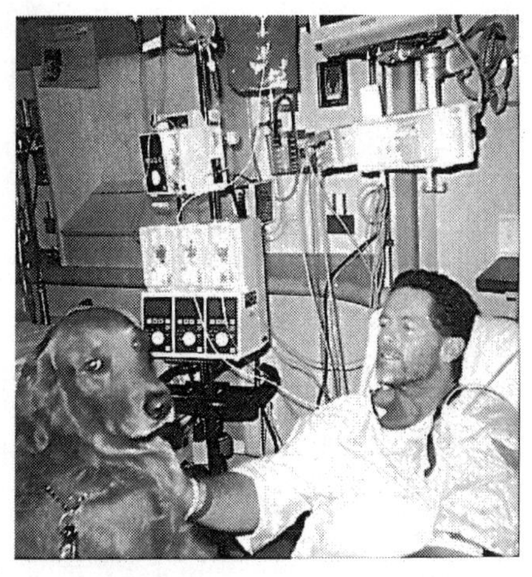

We've been in the ICU for exactly four weeks. TJ has lost almost fifty pounds, and I feel like a pale remnant of myself, existing on crackers and peanut butter provided in the ICU family lounge. When I occasionally take a break and go to the hospital cafeteria to eat, TJ accuses me of having an affair with a doctor that I'm undoubtedly meeting there. It would be laughable if the words didn't hurt so much.

"Look at me," I respond. "First of all, I would never do that. But, again, look at me. I've been sleeping in my clothes and haven't had a full night's sleep since we got here. Plus, I haven't had a shower in almost a week. I'm not having an affair. I just want a bowl of soup, and I don't want to eat it in front of you."

But he persists in throwing verbal assaults about the doctor, who is undoubtedly waiting for me in the cafeteria. It takes me some time to figure out this isn't TJ talking—it's the drugs. Actually, it's one drug. I realize this marked change in his personality began when they started giving him a pain medication called Dilaudid. It has made him angry and paranoid, and, at my request, they change his medication, and his tantrums disappear.

I continue to fill my days by doing everything I can for TJ as the December 18th date we selected for our wedding gets closer. No one can assure me that TJ will be well enough to go home by then or if he'll even live until then. Fevers still plague him, and he's really not improving. It's the most dreadful kind of limbo, two steps forward and two back. Rinse. Repeat.

"Can we just get married in the chapel here at the hospital?" TJ asks me one on one of those two-steps-back days.

"I don't want to get married here," I say without hesitation.

"But why?" The look on his face breaks my heart. I can't tell him the real reason is that I'm afraid he'll give up, like having a target date will give him something to hold on for.

"Because you're going to get better." I look down so he won't see my eyes fill with tears as I try to make myself believe my own words. "Look, I'm addressing wedding invitations. December 18th, see?" I show him the invitations he's seen before.

"See that stack over there? I've got those all stamped, and I'm mailing them tomorrow. I'm even inviting Jean and my brothers. We're getting married at church on December 18th, just like we planned, so start getting better." He's asleep before I finish talking. I'm not sure he's heard a word I said.

I hold on to the hope of a wedding that may never happen, putting together photos for a wedding slide show. The photos reflect the life we had that feels so far away right now. Then the thought hits me, and I start to cry, praying, "God, please let us play this at our wedding and not at a memorial service." And now I'm sobbing. TJ doesn't hear me. I pray God does.

When TJ's been fever-free for six days, I take a half-day break from the hospital and return to our church to work on the Jesus and the Children mural. So often, as I've sat by his bed when things are quiet, I've wondered if the devil thinks he's won by keeping me away from what God has called me to do. I have to prove him wrong. It feels good to be back in the Lord's house and working on His mural while my praise music blares. Take that, devil.

Two days later, on Thanksgiving morning, TJ is released to go home, six weeks and two days after he was admitted. He'll stay with Dad and me so I can care for him. He still can't eat or drink anything, so he carries a backpack containing the pump that continuously pushes TPN, medications, and insulin into his body. The joy on his face as he gets into the car to go home is priceless. Plastic bags of TPN and vials of vitamins and medications are delivered to the house and fill the refrigerator. A home health nurse visits to show me how to measure the various vials of vitamins, medications, and insulin into the bag with a syringe. I'm obsessive, almost to the point of paranoia, triple-checking all the measurements. If I accidentally confuse the dosage of insulin, I could kill him. I also learn how to care for and service the pump that clicks away non-stop, signaling it's working until it beeps for attention or needs fresh batteries. We're so excited he's home as we give thanks over our Thanksgiving dinner of spaghetti and a jar of sauce for Dad and me, and a spoonful of ice chips for TJ. He begs me not to take him back to the hospital when his fever spikes less than twenty-four hours later.

He's readmitted to the ICU with a fever of 102.6. The beeping machines and IV poles filled with various medication bags are back. Again, I hear those words I can no longer bear to hear coming from his doctor's mouth. "There's nothing more we can do. It's up to his body now."

"I'm not accepting that. It's up to God, and we're praying for a miracle if that's all right with you." I reply, and I'm not using my nice girl voice. I'm tired, and I'm frustrated. What I'm feeling doesn't hold a candle to the utter despair coming from TJ. The days pass slowly with the constant battle of spiking fevers and spiking blood sugars as if he's caught in a riptide that keeps pulling him under.

Six days later, and sometime around midnight, TJ's fever spikes to 105.2. His skin is shiny red like he's been burned, and he shivers uncontrollably. His nurse comes in to tell us they are going to put him on ice packs to lower his body temperature. When she leaves the room, he begs me, "Please, don't let them put me on ice. I'm freezing. Please." He speaks through chattering teeth as I put a cold compress on his forehead and remove the blankets he keeps pulling over himself. Nothing I can say will comfort him. We wait for the ice packs as the door to his room remains closed. Why does everything feel so much more hopeless in the dark? I take his hands as I've so often done, "Let's pray,"

TJ's eyes fill with tears, and he closes them, forcing the tears down his cheeks. "I don't know what to pray for anymore."

Now I can't hold back my own tears, ruining the image of being strong for him I've tried to maintain. Closing my eyes, I realize I have no words either, and the only prayer we have is our tears.

That's when the door to his room opens, and a nurse we've never seen walks in. She walks to the foot of his bed, lays her hands on his feet, and says, "Always remember, all things are possible through Jesus Christ who strengthens me." She smiles and walks out of the room, closing the door behind her. We will never see her again.

I have now found my words, "Jesus just spoke to you; now don't you give up on me." We pray, still crying, thanking God for His promises, His Son through whom all things are possible, and for hearing those wordless prayers that our tears contain.

TJ never has to spend time on those ice packs. His temperature immediately starts to go down and is completely gone within six hours. When the doctors tell us they can't explain his sudden improvement, we tell them we can: "All things are possible through Jesus Christ who strengthens me."

TJ is discharged from the hospital nine days later, fifty-nine days after he was first admitted. This time, I feel confident that we won't be returning to the hospital until his colon resection, which is scheduled for February. He still can't eat and will continue to be fed with TPN through a central line until his surgery.

Leaving the hospital this time, the world feels different—it's turning again. That night, as I listen to the gentle whir of the TPN pump, I thank God for being with us through this journey and for all His answers to prayer. This chapter is ending, and our wedding will take place in a week. Thank you, Lord.

Marriage as a Testimony

On December 18th, one week after TJ is discharged from the hospital, we are married just as we'd planned. A week before the wedding, I ask Dad if he will give me away. He laughs and says, "I keep trying, but you keep coming back!" Resulting in one of my most memorable laughing fits. Laughing feels so good after the laughter drought we've been through.

As I walk down the aisle of our church, holding Dad's arm, I scan the faces for Jean and my brothers. They're not there, which hurts, but nothing can steal the joy from this moment. Our marriage serves as a testimony to the power of the prayers of all those who now fill the church and our thankfulness to our God who hears them.

TJ meets me at the altar, carrying his backpack, which holds the pump that still forces TPN into his body. During communion, he chews the tiny wafer, pulverizing it. He's still not allowed to eat or drink, but he breaks the rules for communion. We say our vows and mean every word with a kind of "been there, done that" confidence. "*in sickness and in health, to love and to cherish, till death us do part.*" We now have a pretty good understanding of what that truly means. This time we're doing marriage right, with God as our foundation. We love each other and love Jesus even more.

Two months later, TJ ends up having two surgeries to repair his perforated colon, and at long last, he can eat, something he hasn't done in over four months.

There's no way to fully express our gratitude to God for TJ's complete recovery and for each person and medical professional God put in our lives during that time. While we wouldn't volunteer to repeat those fifty-nine days in the ICU and the surgeries that followed, we wouldn't trade for anything the way the Lord used that journey to grow our faith and the faith of those around us. The scars on TJ's body will forever serve as a reminder and a testament of God's healing, and we will forever be thankful.

The Year of the Big Ugly

2008 will go down as The Year of the Big Ugly. Sadness and loss will strike almost every month and no other year has been more painful, before or since. Illness, dismemberment, and death will all be a part of this dreadful year, a year that would take a whole other book to describe, but I'll give you a brief synopsis.

It starts with my real estate broker filing for bankruptcy without warning. You're probably thinking, big whoop-de-do, and you'd be correct, but hindsight is always 20/20. Regardless, I start the new year thinking, "*This is the worst way to start a new year*." Little do I know, it's nothing compared to what's coming.

Between March and August, one catastrophe follows another. My nephew dies unexpectedly; TJ's seventeen-year-old daughter has a car accident and suffers multiple injuries, including a broken neck and loss of her arm; TJ's mom falls twice, breaking one hip and then the other; I have a complete hysterectomy after cancer cells are found during my annual exam; and TJ has surgery to repair a disc in his back which results in a staph infection in his spine, requiring a second surgery a couple months later. Then in September, Dad's oncologist informs us his chemo treatments are no longer working.

Dad has fought his cancer battle for twelve years with not so much as a single complaint, though the pain has been severe at times. In 2005, just months after TJ's colon resection, we learned that Dad's prostate cancer had spread to his colon, requiring a colon resection and chemotherapy. A few months later, his oncologist suggested we call in hospice. Dad just giggled and asked, "Why? Are they going to caddy for me?" Dad was still golfing three or four times a week, and I told him, "The doctors don't know how long you have; only God holds that date book, so you keep on golfing and enjoying life." Which is precisely what he did. But now, three years later, the cancer has spread to his liver and lungs, and we are out of treatment options.

Dad is fading away. I've been watching it happen. It's not a surprise. So at his next appointment, when his oncologist suggests we call in hospice, I know this time he's right. Dad's only response is, "Well, Doc, I wanted to live to see the Cubs win the pennant, but I guess I can't live forever, can I?"

He and his doctor laugh, but I can only offer half a smile as the dam behind my eyes threatens to burst. I feel my throat close as sobs strain to break free, and I inhale slowly as Dad reaches over and pats my arm. I should be comforting him, but that's not what happens.

His oncologist says, "Hospice will call to set up visits for you," and this time, Dad doesn't ask if they'll be caddying for him. He knows it's time, too. He hasn't been strong enough to golf in over four months.

We drive home, talking about nothing of substance. I'm afraid I'll lose my grip if I speak the words we've just heard. Dad doesn't seem sad. He's like he always is, happy and reading all the billboards and traffic signs out loud to me, as he's done every time we've made this trip like it's just another day.

"No P," he says as we pass a no parking sign signified by the letter P in a circle with a line through it. "No peeing there, li'l sweetheart." I've heard this joke at least a hundred times and thought I had tired of it. But now I know I won't hear it much longer and would give anything to hear it a hundred times more.

"Nope, Daddy, not there." I squeak. It's the only sound I can make.

When we get home, Dad goes to his room to watch a ball game on TV, and I go into my closet, fall on my knees, and sob as my eyes give up the torrent of tears I've been holding back. When the sobs ebb, I remain seated on the closet floor and pray, "God, I'm asking You for Dad's healing again, but it looks like You may have decided it's time for him to come home. Thank You for giving me as much time with him as

You have. But this is harder than I thought it would be. If you can spare a miracle, I'm asking for one now. If not, please don't let him suffer." And I'm crying again.

I drag myself to the sink to splash cold water on my face, washing off the mascara trail that's running down my cheeks. Looking in the mirror, I barely recognize the face looking back at me. I know when I wake up in the morning, my eyes will be swollen shut from the crying. I go to Dad's room and hear a ballgame playing on his TV. Take a few deep breaths, I knock on his door. There's no way to hide the evidence of my crying jag, which is hard for me because I still want to be strong for him.

"Hey, li'l sweetheart," he says as he opens the door, and I put my arms around him.

"I'm scared, Daddy. I don't want you to go." I can't say "die," and the sobbing starts all over again.

He holds me and pats my back. "It's all going to be okay. You're going to be okay." With my arms around him, I feel the bones in his back. He's lost more weight than I'd realized. My mind goes back to those times as a child when I curled up in his lap. If only I could turn back time.

October 2, 2008—Dad lost his long battle with cancer at 0630 hours this morning; that's 6:30 am for any non-military types. Even through the sadness, I thank God that Dad could live with me for the last 7½ years of his life. He brought me so much joy and companionship, but my heart is aching at the sight of his empty chair.

Cancer didn't get the best of Dad until the very end. His joy of life continued as hospice visited daily, and all the nurses love him. When he tells me he's going to take his golf cart to see all his old golf buddies before they tee off the following day, I know this is really a trip to say goodbye. He hasn't driven his golf cart in a few months, so I ask, "Do you think you're strong enough to drive your cart?"

"Geez, Amy, I'm not feeble," is his reply.

To which I respond, "Well, yeah, Dad, you kinda are." Instantly regretting my words, I try to cover them with, "How 'bout if, before you go tomorrow, you take me for a spin around the block in your cart so we can make sure you don't have any trouble?"

"Okay." He sounds defeated, and that's not how I want him to feel.

"I'd like that. You haven't taken me for a ride since I was a kid!" I try to make it sound like that's the reason we're doing this, but I'm not fooling him.

The next morning, he sneaks out of the house like a teenager, and I can't help but laugh when I tell TJ, "Well, Dad's taken the cart out. I hope he'll be okay."

"Ah, let him go." TJ understands.

But I don't want to let him go —not ever.

When Dad gets home, he's proud of the trick he played on me. This will be the last time I'll ever hear his giggle because the following day, the giggling stops. No one on earth will ever hear it again. His decline happens rapidly, like a switch that's been flipped or like he's jumped off a cliff.

When I come home from work that afternoon, he doesn't yell, "Who dat?" like he always does when I walk through the door, and I know something's wrong. I find him sitting in his recliner, still in his pajamas. His coffee cup, still filled with morning coffee, sits cold on the table beside him, and the TV is blaring. I'm mad at myself for spending the whole day at the office, leaving him alone. He doesn't appear to know I'm even there as he fiddles with a button on his pajamas.

Turning down the TV, I say, "Whatcha doin', Dad?"

He doesn't look up. "I have to fix this."

"Fix what?" I ask and reach down to the button. He gently bats my hand away. Something is wrong. Very, very wrong. The daddy I knew is gone, just like that.

The next day, every bit of my soul aches as Dad cries out, "Please help me," as his pain intensifies. I crush the morphine in a spoon with water and carefully place it under his tongue. For some reason, he doesn't want to stay in his bed, so I sit on the floor next to the couch where he lies. Holding his hand, I struggle with the overwhelming sense of helplessness as I pray. That night, I pile pillows in front of the couch in case he rolls off in his sleep, and I sleep on the loveseat next to him. Hospice will deliver a hospital bed to our living room the following day.

Just three days after I found him sitting in his chair next to his cup of cold coffee, the hospice nurse tells me he has little time left. My daughter and I sit on either side of his bed, each holding one of his hands as his pulse weakens. I know it's time to tell him it's okay to go, but it's the last thing I want to do. I take a few deep breaths and stroke the back of his hand and the side of his face. Then I whisper to him with a heavy voice, "Daddy, you taught us to be so strong. We'll be okay." My tears fall on his arm, and I gently wipe each one away as it falls. I feel like I'm lying to him. No part of me feels like it will be okay ever again.

"Jesus is waiting to take all your pain away, Daddy. Mom is waiting for you, too, and she'll probably ask you what took you so long. Now I have to tell you it's okay to go. When you get to heaven, make sure you save the seat next to you for me, okay? I love you, Daddy."

Just two minutes pass as we hold him, and he takes his last breath peacefully, quietly, and surrounded by love. Ten seconds later, he squeezes our hands one last time, which I know is probably just a reflex, but I can't help but feel it's his "See ya later, alligator." I whisper a reply with the words he taught me, "After a while, crocodile." My little daddy is gone, and life as I knew it will never be the same.

They say time heals, but I fear it will take longer than I thought for this aching in my chest to stop. I can hear the clock ticking in our house, which is now hauntingly quiet without the sounds of Dad's beloved baseball, football, or golf game playing on the TV. Everywhere I turn, I see remnants of him. His glasses and crossword puzzle books that I refuse to remove from the kitchen table, all the sticky notes he's written to himself to remind him of things he'll never do, and his chair, his empty chair —that hurts most of all.

TJ asks me if he can bring me anything else as I sit in Dad's chair that first night after I said goodbye. I'm wearing Dad's robe, holding the sweater he wore every day and the pillow from his bed that still smells like him. Unless he can wake me up from this horrible dream, there's nothing he can do. Will I ever stop crying? It sure doesn't feel like it.

As the weeks pass, my crying is no longer a daily event, but it can come on suddenly, like when I walk into the house, and Dad doesn't yell, "Who dat?"—but somehow I hear him anyway. When I find one of his cough drop wrappers, I pick it up, knowing that it was last held by Dad, and squeeze my hand around it as the tears fall.

One day, TJ walks into Dad's bedroom while I'm packing up his clothes and things. He finds me sitting on Dad's bed, holding a cup with Dad's false teeth in it and crying my eyes out.

"What can I do?" he asks, sitting down beside me.

"I don't know what to do with his teeth," I sob.

TJ puts his arms around me. "Just leave them in his bathroom for now." And I do. He reminds me it will get easier, and now, sixteen years later, I can tell you that's true, for the most part. I still have his glasses bearing his fingerprints on the lenses, his wallet just as it was the day he died, complete with two five-dollar bills tucked inside. Oh, and of course, the sweater he wore every day. When I need one of his hugs, I wrap the arms of his sweater around me and close my eyes, imagining him. I kept his last can of Old Milwaukee Light Beer until a friend came over and grabbed it out of the fridge. I didn't notice until I heard him pull the pop top off and watched as he took a big swig.

"How's that beer?" I asked him, noticing the funny look on his face.

"It's a little flat." He said.

"No doubt. It's about four years old. It was my dad's last beer."

My friend was mortified like he had somehow destroyed something sacred, but I couldn't get upset. The look on his face was worth it, and Dad would have laughed.

Sights, sounds, smells, songs—I guess they'll always trigger memories of my little daddy. I still can't watch a Popeye or a Woody Woodpecker cartoon without tearing up, and the theme song from M.A.S.H., which he watched every night, does the same. His teeth, though. I have to tell you; I never could throw them away because they felt like a part of his smile. So one day, I put them in a box lined with tissue paper and buried them in the yard like a dead bird. And when I tapped the last bit of dirt over them, I swear I heard Daddy giggling.

But back to the rest of the story —The days after Dad dies, TJ is back in the hospital for the second surgery to treat his spinal infection. I leave the hospital after his surgery, taking that familiar route I took almost exactly four years earlier when TJ was in the ICU. It's also the same route I drove for Dad's chemo treatments. I'm driving home to feed the dog because Dad's no longer there to do it. It was one of his chores that he loved to do. And that's when I come apart. My heart hurts so bad it feels like it's literally breaking over the loss of my dad and now being back in the hospital with TJ. I struggle to see the road through my crying fit. (I know… this whole year, I seem to be crying.)

I turn on my favorite Christian radio station and pray while driving, "Lord, I'm at the bottom, and I don't know how much more I can take. Dad is gone. TJ is sick. But You know all that. It's been an awful year. Please let me know Dad is there with You and that You're in control of this mess down here. "Please, God. Please, God," I sob.

That's when the radio announcer introduces "There Will Be a Day," a new song by Jeremy Camp that I've never heard before. As I listen to the lyrics with tears still flowing, Jeremy's voice echoes every emotion I'm feeling, but then he delivers a message of hope: one day we will meet Jesus, our tears will be wiped away, and there will be no more pain.

Though God has often spoken to me through music, this moment feels different. As I listen, I experience a profound shift—a physical sensation of weariness and sadness lifting from my body, something words alone can't describe. A deep peace fills me, and I know Dad is with Jesus. Once again, my prayer has been answered.

When I add Dad's date of death to my calendar journal, where I record all significant dates, I see another anniversary written on that date, twenty-seven years earlier. October 2, 1981, was a day I still remember as one of the saddest in my life. I've told you that story, remember? It was the day I waved goodbye to Dad at the airport on my way to Arizona to find Jean —it takes my breath away as it all comes together like a flashing neon sign. There are just too many of these "coincidences" in my life to believe they're random, and I can't help but reflect on God's presence in my life.

Take, for example, the number twenty-seven. February 27 was the date of my birth; October 27 was the date my adoption was final; and June 27 was the date of my return to the Lord—that Sunday when He dimmed the lights so I could finally see. There are many others, but these are the biggest ones. So when I see that number reflected again in the date God called Dad home, exactly twenty-seven years after I began my adoption search, I can almost hear God saying, *"I've been right here all along, Amy. You've never walked alone."*

I notice things like this a lot more now, and, like a wink from God, they always make me smile. I call them God-incidences because believing they are random would take more faith.

Have you ever noticed things like this and brushed them off with words like, "What a coincidence."? Let me take this opportunity to say —maybe not.

I encourage you to keep your eyes and your heart open for these little winks. God would love to remind you that He's walking with you, too.

Making Peace With Truth

Eight years, which feel like a lifetime, have passed since I've seen or spoken to Jean. It's 2012, she would now be seventy-four years old if she's still alive. I assume she is, but I can't be sure. I've thought about her and our relationship a lot over that time and have come to understand that my relationship with her was always fragile, like a tissue paper flower that even a drop of rain can wound. In reality, our relationship would only survive if she never showed any signs of rejecting me. I could never think she loved me unconditionally. Each disagreement or misunderstanding signified rejection and chipped away at that. It might not have been that way for her, but maybe it was. How would we ever know? We never discussed our pain.

For eight years, I've prayed about the situation while trying to convince myself that I've forgiven her, but as soon as I think about what happened, the anger returns. My forgiveness is a lie. I tell God my side of the story repeatedly, explaining why I feel the way I do as if I can convince Him I'm right, she's wrong, and He'll let me off the hook about his whole forgiveness thing. I'm having another one of these conversations with God while riding my bike one day, and I ask Him again, "How can I forgive her, Lord? I forgave her for giving me up, and after I found her, I was always there for her with anything she ever needed. After all I'd done for her, she just turned her back on me and rejected me all over again. How can I ever forgive her for that?"

Then I feel His words in my soul, "*You mean like I forgave you for giving Me up after all I'd done for you? You mean, like I've always been there for you with anything you've needed? Like I forgave you after you turned your back on Me and all those times you rejected Me all over again? Like that, you mean?*"

I pull over to the curb, get off my bike, and sit down in the grass. Shaken at the truth of what I'd just "heard." (I'm still waiting for a word to describe how I hear from God. A combination of feeling and hearing, not quite either, but both at the same time.) The revelation of my hypocrisy is blinding. I whisper, "Lord, forgive me," and in that moment, I truly forgive her. I feel unbound. Unforgiveness is no longer strangling my heart. For the very first time, I am at peace with my birth mother.

I call Jean right away to apologize for my part in the whole mess.

Now, wouldn't that be the perfect ending for this story? But that's not what happens. I don't call her. I don't go to see her. I don't do anything, except get back on my bike and ride home. Because even though I've forgiven her, my heart fears being rejected again, and that wall remains standing. I tell myself I would welcome her back into my life with open arms if she makes the first move, and I believe that to be true. But me? I'm not giving her an invitation she can decline. That wall is fine right where it is.

Is that the right way to feel? I pray, "Lord, I truly forgive Jean. Really, I do. But I'm wondering, do I have to tell her I'm sorry and have forgiven her? Do I have to invite her back into my life again? Lord, please let me know what You want me to do. And, oh, by the way, thank You for continuing to love me in spite of myself."

There's no lightning bolt realization of what I'm supposed to do. I feel at peace with doing nothing, so I take that as the answer to my prayer.

Three months pass, and one day, I notice a missed call on my phone. I vaguely recognize the number, but it's not in my contacts list. When I click on the voicemail, I hear her voice, "Hi, it's me, your long-lost mother, just calling to say hello. Call me back if you'd like to. Okay then. Bye."

Without hesitation, I return her call and she answers, "Well, hello!"

"Hi, Mom! How are you?"

"I'm fine. How are you?"

"I'm good. So what's new?"

Really, that's exactly how it goes. It's as if those eight years never happened. Just like that, she's back in my life, but those years didn't simply evaporate—they were thrown away, and we can never get them back. We never discuss that black hole in our relationship or the significant events that took place during that time. There's no talk of my wedding, TJ's near-death experience, or the Year of the Big Ugly, including the death of my dad. She doesn't ask, and I don't feel any need to tell her. The reverse is true as well. I never ask about her last eight years, either. Maybe if we had talked about how we ended up where we did or maybe examined that list of things she didn't like about me, our relationship might have healed with fewer scars and perhaps even grown stronger. I don't know. Maybe not. Instead, we start over with generic happy talk, like the kind you have with the cashier at Walmart. We're identical in our handling or not handling of the situation. The forgiveness feels sincere, but the walls around my heart still stand. I do, however, put in a gate that allows Jean access to some parts of it. Honestly, I think Jean does the same.

A year later, everything falls apart, but this time it's beyond any of our control. It starts with small things for her, like not remembering words. Jean says it's like the word is right there, floating in front of her face, but she can't grasp it. I take her to play bingo, and she struggles to find the numbers they are calling, and I have to cover them for her. She attributes it to "getting old," but I know it's more than that. The Alzheimer's that took her mother's memory is now taking Jean's.

Leaving my house after a visit one day, Jean can't remember how to put her car in reverse. I watch as she pulls into my neighbor's driveway to turn around and just sits there. I go to the car and she tells me the car won't move. She mashes the accelerator to the floor with the car in park to prove it. I yell over the roaring engine, "Stop! Stop!" which she eventually does, and I move her to the passenger seat as I get behind the wheel. I put the car in reverse, and it backs up just like it should. She swears the gear shift has been getting stuck and agrees to follow me to the service station, but as I get into my car, she takes off. She's traveling at least fifteen miles over the speed limit as I try to pass her, hoping I can get in front of her to slow her down. Pulling in front of her and gradually reducing my speed, she suddenly speeds up and almost plows into the back of my car. Swerving to get around me, she speeds through the intersection as the traffic light turns red and continues down the road. Five minutes later, I'm pulling up to her house, thankful to see her car intact and sitting in the garage. I enter the house and ask her why she was driving so fast and didn't follow me to the service station. She has no idea what I'm talking about.

I let my brother Danny know what happened with Jean, and within a couple of months, he has sold her home, and she's living with him and his family. I'm not a part of any decision-making for Jean's medical care or any other decisions for that matter, and I'm okay with that. When Jean came back into my life in 2012, my brothers did not, and it still hurts. I speak to Danny only while she's living with him, and I'm scheduling a time to visit her at his house. He and I hug, and it's all very cordial, but it goes no further than that. I last saw or spoke to my other brother, Tom, in 2004.

Tell Your Story

This is the point in my journey that I shared with you in the Preface of this book. That fateful spring day in 2017, when I felt God say, "*Tell your story*." This is the rest of the story of how this book came to be:

I had come to the end of myself and felt I could not do life as I knew it anymore. Don't get me wrong, I didn't have a death wish. I was not suicidal. I just felt like I didn't want to "do" anymore. I didn't want to sell another house or do anything I'd been doing. I knew there was something I was supposed to be doing, but I didn't know what it was. I felt I was in some kind of spiritual echo chamber, calling out to God but only hearing my echo. This is when TJ suggested I go for one of my Jesus walks, something I did often. Listening to my praise music, I would walk miles praising God and asking Him what He wanted me to do. But He had remained silent as far as I could tell.

That day, I forgot my earbuds, so I walked and prayed in silence, without a soundtrack, and that's when I "heard" Him say, ***"I've told you what I want you to do. Tell your story."***

With my thoughts spinning, I pull out my phone and call TJ. When he answers, the words come gushing out of my mouth in a single sentence without pause or breath, "I know what I have to do! I just heard God say, 'Tell your story.' It feels so clear and so right. I think we should sell our real estate business and move to the mountains so I can focus on writing because there's no way I can write working all these hours, and yeah, I know it'll mean some adjustments, but—"

"Where are you?" He interrupts and may be wondering if I've had some kind of nervous breakdown.

"I'm walking."

"Just come home."

"But it was the most amazing thing! I can't even describe it!"

"Okay. Come home, and we'll talk."

I turn around and head home while I contemplate the words still running through my head: "I've told you what I want you to do." When exactly did He do that? I ponder all the prayers and how I thought God had remained silent, but now He's telling me He's already told me what He wants me to do.

Then it hits me like another lightning bolt. For years, whenever I shared bits and pieces of my story, many have said, "You need to write a book!"

"Yeah, yeah," I'd respond, "Someday when I have time." A "someday" I knew would probably never come.

Could it be that sometimes, when God speaks, he uses someone else's mouth?

My thoughts then move to another question. I had prayed for an answer for so long, and now I wonder, "W*hy did He wait so long to answer?"* Then I think about my prayer time, which is always filled with my words, like a one-way conversation. Have I ever been still and just listened for Him? The answer to that question is a resounding NO. I have not been still, and I say every prayer with one eye on God and one eye on my to-do list. My squirrel brain often interrupts my prayers, and I wrap up my time with the Lord with a quick "Amen." Twelve to fourteen-hour workdays consume my time. In the battle between *Doing* and *Being*, *Doing* always wins. When an opportunity comes along to "be" and not "do," browsing my phone, reading my books, working on my crafts, or watching my favorite TV shows, steal every spare moment I have. No, that's a lie. Nothing steals my time; I give it away.

Of course, God can get our attention in any way He wants to, but maybe when we ask God a question that we genuinely want an answer to, it's our responsibility to actually listen for His answer. He shouldn't have to make the earth shake. My heart is still racing, and my mind is in overdrive as I approach our house. I realize just how crazy I must have sounded to TJ, so when I get home, I'm a little surprised he's not sitting in the driveway with the car running, ready to take me to the hospital. He meets me at the door, takes me in his arms, and asks, "Are you okay?" I stand in that embrace for what feels like too long, willing myself not to cry while trying to catch the words swirling in my brain like dandelion seeds in the wind. Which words will make him understand what just happened and this huge next step I feel we have to take? Every word seems inadequate to describe what I've just experienced.

When I'm finally able to speak, I tell the story again, this time in complete sentences, spoken calmly and rationally. When I'm done speaking, I brace myself for his logical response that is sure to come, complete with all the reasons we can't retire and move to the mountains, no matter what I thought I heard. But that's not what happens. To my utter amazement, he doesn't blink an eye when I'm done speaking. Instead, he smiles and says, "Okay. So what do we do next?"

Two months later, we've sold our home, sold our business to TJ's daughter, and are moving to our cabin in the mountains. Leaving behind a home I've loved has always been bittersweet, and it's no different this time. As I walk through it for the last time, I run my hand over each surface as my eyes try to absorb every molecule of its existence. But it's not the details of the structure that fill my senses; it's the fifteen years of memories each square inch contains. I see our wedding reception here, surrounded by those we love and the beginning of our life together as husband and wife. Echos of the laughter of our children and grandchildren and even dad's giggle ricochet off the walls. I can almost feel my dad's hand in mine, and the faint sound of my voice choked with tears, saying, "It's ok to go, Daddy," as he took his last breath in the space where I stand. I turn slowly as if trying to absorb the last wisp of him. It all comes flooding back: the joyful times and the times during life's trials when I fell to my knees when only God could help.

My mind fills with memories of the souls that shared this space, if even for a few hours, and those who now only live in anyone's memory: my dad, TJ's parents, and even my little dog, Merf. I feel them all beside me as I walk through every room. How long has it been since I hugged them? I can't hold back the tears as it feels like I'm leaving the last little piece of them behind. I see my daughters holding my grandchildren and TJ's daughters laughing with their grandma over a story she's told. I see every family member and friend I've shared meals, laughs, and tears with. Like some kind of surreal movie, I see the joy of my grandchildren as they open their Christmas presents. I hear their laughter as they search for their Easter eggs with the treasure map I made.

Walking through each room, I thank God for the blessing of this home, for every breath taken within these walls, and for each tear shed that strengthened us. Finally, I ask God to be with the new owners and that the memories they create in this space will bring them as much joy. And then it hits me. I'm not leaving anything or anyone behind. My memories don't live here. Every precious memory lives within me… easily transportable and easily accessible…no packing tape required. So I wipe my tears as I stand in the doorway and take one final survey of the empty room. The ghosts have gone, neatly packed in my heart, as I turn and gently close the door behind me, turning the key for one last time.

Goodbye house. Thanks for the memories.

Two months later, we've settled into our new home in the mountains, and I'm ready to begin working on this task God has given me. That's when the doubting begins. The voices in my head, dripping with sarcasm, accuse me. "*So you've given up a lucrative career to pursue something you have no qualifications for. Good job. Who do you think is going to be interested in your story? You're not a writer. You've never written anything in your life. God spoke to you. Right. Gimme a break. What a joke.*" And yes, I actually hear them laughing.

After much prayer and when the voices seem to be quiet, I push all my doubts aside, and on May 12, 2017, I write my first words. I write, and I write, and the next day I question everything I wrote the day before and delete almost all of it. I continue to write even as I wonder if I've imagined this task I believe God has called me to do. "*Who do you think you are?*" is all I can hear in my head as I write words that are flat and lackluster.

Have you ever tried to accomplish anything when all you feel is doubt in your abilities? So I close my laptop and walk away to regroup and refocus. I spend more time walking in the woods, praying for inspiration than I do actually writing. I ask God, "Was that You I heard? Is this really what You want me to do, Lord?" When I don't hear an answer in my soul, I listen for His voice in the wind. Hey, at least now I'm listening. Weeks pass as the first words of my story sit on a laptop that eventually loses its charge.

In the meantime, TJ and I are searching for our new church, and eventually, we will visit the one that will become our church home. The pastor's message on our first visit ends with the words, "Tell your story." Those three words fill the large screens at the front of the church. Could my answer be any clearer?

Determined, I pick up where I left off, trying to rescue a book that now reads like "Green Eggs and Ham" without the poetry. I'm stuck in quicksand a few days later, and the words won't come. This must be what they call writer's block. I still don't consider myself a writer, but the block I can identify with. So I close my laptop again, leaving it and my story to sit while they both gather dust. I tell myself lies like, "If God had wanted me to write, He would have made it easier." But even as I say it, I know that's not true. I don't know of a single story where God asked someone to do something that was easy. Weeks turn into months as the task God has given me sits untouched on my laptop. But it's not out of sight, out of mind. It scratches the back of my consciousness, urging, prodding, and cajoling. My guilt is yelling loud and clear, but it's not enough. The task feels overwhelming, and the story God told me to tell sits undone, buried in my excuses.

Then one day, while I'm flipping through channels on the TV (a favorite pastime that should be called "lost time"), I stop to watch an interview with a man who left his lucrative sports career. Anyone who knows me knows I was born without a sports gene. Name any sport, from football to fencing; I have zero interest in any of them. But still, I stop and watch this guy. I have no idea who he is or what sport he played. I have no interest in why he left his sports career, yet I'm mesmerized by what he's saying and have no desire to change the channel. Ten minutes into the interview, he's asked why he gave up his sports career to write a book. He answers, "Fame stopped mattering. I was miserable. Something was missing. Then one day I heard God say, '*Tell your story.*'"

The words are like a dagger to my heart, and I'm now bent over my lap with my head on my knees. *How many times does God have to tell me? What is wrong with me?* If I could find a rock to crawl under, I would. So I open my computer, write like a maniac, and complete my book, right? Wrong. This writing journey will take seven years. Sometimes, I sprint and jump over hurdles, but more often, I'm limping along and stumbling over my doubts as I try to make it perfect.

As my writing stalls for what feels like the hundredth time, I see a vivid image in my mind. My time on earth has ended, and I'm standing before God when He asks, *So Amy, how's that book coming along?"*

Can you imagine? That humiliating picture brings a brand new realization. When God asks us to do something, He doesn't require perfection. All He asks for is our obedience. He doesn't tell us to worry about the end result—He'll take care of that.

I realize now that my trust was misplaced from the very beginning. I relied solely on my own abilities or my perceived lack of them instead of placing my trust in God. When my skills fell short, my confidence faltered, creating a perfect storm of frustration and failure. But when I finally step aside and place my trust in Him, the words flow effortlessly like never before.

When DNA Speaks

I hear about Ancestry.com and how its DNA matching could connect me with potential relatives. Could this be the key to finding out more about my birth father? He crosses my mind occasionally, and I'm still curious about him. So, I order the DNA kit, spit into the provided vial, and send it off.

A few weeks later, my DNA test results are in and I see "Neal" family matches on my account and at the top, "High Probability - First Cousin - Neal." It's fascinating and I spend hours reviewing all the relatives and ancestors and their photos. I find no mention of a Charles.

I study the face of "High-Probability-First-Cousin." Do we bear any resemblance? Not really. Should I reach out to her? That's going against all the rules of keeping the secret, but is it really my birth father's secret if he doesn't even know I exist? Still, the questions I've visited before are back; *how far do I want to go with this? Do I want to take the chance of kicking a hornet's nest? Who knows what I'll find?*

The questions do not differ from when I started my search for Jean, and all the what-ifs almost derailed me. Here I am again.

As I weigh my options, this time, I know without a doubt that if God wants me to find my birth father, I will. So I write a message to "High-Probability-First-Cousin."

I was adopted at birth, and I found my birth mother thirty-four years ago. She told me her pregnancy was the result of a brief relationship with a man named Charles Neal. To the best of my knowledge, he does not know I exist. My DNA results list you as a "high probability first cousin," so I became hopeful that you may hold some answers to my questions.

I am not looking for a relationship with my birth father, nor do I want to disrupt his life with this information. However, I would love to know my heritage, family origin, health history, etc. I would also love to be able to pass the information along to my daughters and grandchildren, as that piece of their puzzle is also missing. Please let me know if you would be interested in helping me. Thank you so much. Amy

I review the note 117 times, or so it seems. Finally satisfied, I close my eyes and pray, "God, Your will be done," then click the send button. Here we go.

I check my inbox every day. Nothing. A month passes, then another—still nothing. Well, maybe this isn't in God's plan and, honestly, a part of me is relieved. I stop checking the website for weeks at a time. Then, seven months after sending the letter, I log on and find one message in my inbox that, coincidently, had just arrived the day before. It's from "High-Probability-First-Cousin." I open it and read:

"So sorry for the delay in responding. I would be happy to connect if you are still interested in doing so. I have an uncle Charlie. He's my father's brother. Let me know if you are still interested in connecting."

Maybe the length of time between my introductory letter and her response is a good thing because I feel no caution when I type a response and hit the send button. After a series of emails between us, I find out that my birth father is eighty years old and the town where he was last known to be living.

When she leads me to the Facebook page of Charles' younger brother, Jerry, I spend hours stalking his page, an open book brimming with family photos. They look like a normal family if a family can look normal. Then I hit the mother lode, a series of photos of my birth father labeled "Charlie." And, just like I did with Jean's photos when I was eleven, I study every detail of these photos. Another prayer has been answered. I finally know what my birth father looks like. My resemblance to him in some of the photos is startling. I have always looked so much like Jean. I never thought I could look anything like my birth father, but when I see his baby photo, that all changes.

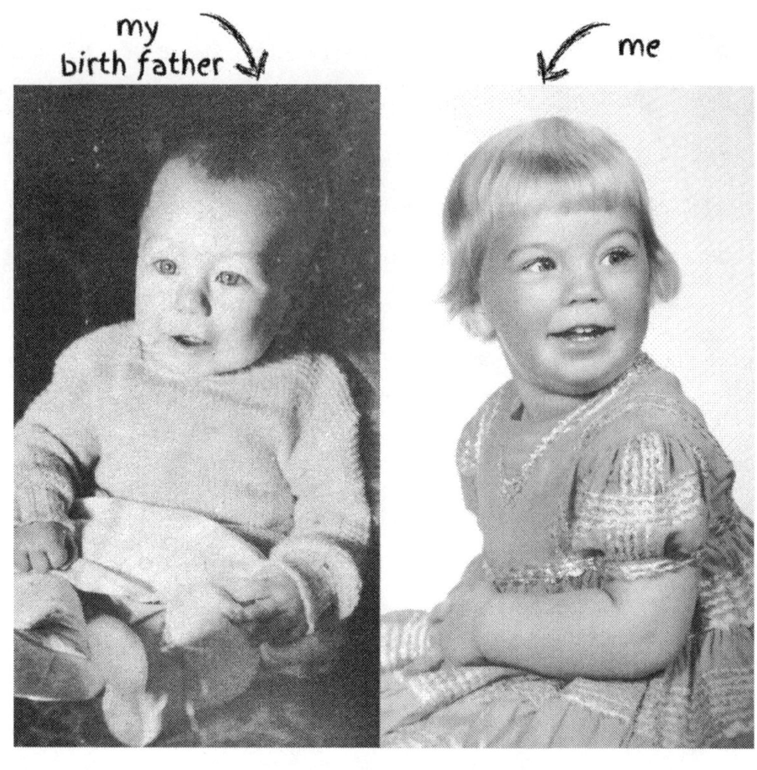

I pay for a background check to make sure he's not an ax murderer or anything and also come up with a likely address. So now what? The same old arguments arise. Arguments that I'm actually quite tired of. I never thought I wanted a relationship with him, but now that a possible relationship seems within reach, how can I not try? So after almost a month of staring at his photos, I write a letter to my birth father.

Dear Charles,

I really hesitated sending you this letter as I'm sure it will be a bit of a shock, and it is not my intent to cause you any anxiety. My name is Amy Jones. I was born in 1959 to Jean Vazquez, from Superior, Arizona. I was adopted at birth but found Jean thirty-five years ago. When I found her, she told me that she knew my birth father very briefly and that his name was Charles Neal, who was a friend of her cousin's. The first thing she said to me when I found her was, "You have your father's eyes" (blue vs. her brown). She also said that my birth father didn't know I existed and that she had no idea where he was.

I recently had my DNA tested through ancestry.com, and, to my amazement, it linked several first and second cousins to me. Through this research, it became clear that you are my birth father.

Please know that while I would love to get to know you, I will understand if this is not something you want to do. I expect nothing from you, but I felt you deserved to know about the family you have.

I was raised by two wonderful and loving parents and am happily married with two daughters and four grandchildren. I have included some photos for you so that you can have a glimpse of this family you never knew you had.

I have always wondered about you and any extended family I may have and would love to meet you someday. If this news makes you happy, I welcome a phone call or email.

If you choose not to respond, I respect that as well. With love, your daughter, Amy

I print out and label some photos of me, Mom and Dad, Jean, and my daughters and grandchildren to include with the letter. I still cringe when I type "adoptive mother" and "adoptive father," but in this situation, it seems necessary. To ensure no one but Charles opens the envelope, the clerk at the post office advises Restricted Delivery. He stamps a big, red "**Private and Restricted–To Be Opened By Addressee Only"** all over the envelope, front and back. Charles will have to sign and show ID to receive the envelope. Well, that ought to do it. Of course, if he takes delivery and his wife or anyone else sees those warnings, that won't cause any curiosity at all, will it? And if he has a heart condition — well, you know. I request a delivery receipt and say another prayer, and it's out of my hands. Now I wait.

The following week, I receive the returned envelope that is now stamped "Undeliverable. No such address." What? How can that be? I was so sure. Again, now what? Maybe this just isn't meant to be.

Attempted Delivery

I've come too far to give up now, so I pull out all the stops and decide to send it to Charles' brother, Jerry, who has been easy to locate based on the information on his Facebook page and tax records. He's living less than a four-hour drive from me.

Once again, I'm violating all the rules of privacy that pertain to birth parents, but whatever. I put the unopened envelope into another envelope and include a note:

Dear Jerry, I have some important information for your brother, Charles, which I tried to mail to him. As you can see, it came back undeliverable, so I'm hoping you can help me by getting it to him. Thank you, Amy

I request a delivery receipt from the postal service, this time with live notifications of delivery or attempted delivery. And with a prayer, it's out of my hands again.

Two days later, I receive notification, "Delivery Attempted, 1 of 3." Drat. The next day, "Delivery Attempted, 2 of 3." I'm disappointed, but decide that if this delivery is unsuccessful, I will put the idea of contacting my birth father to rest and I'm completely at peace with that decision.

The next day, I receive notification. "*Delivery Confirmed. 2:14 pm.*"

My heart races. Well, now I've done it. No turning back. Will Jerry forward the envelope? Does he have a relationship with his brother, or is Charles even alive? Will Jerry leave the envelope sealed, or will he rip it open and maybe set it on fire? I may hear nothing more than what I'm hearing now, my heartbeat pounding in my ears.

Less than an hour later, I receive a message via Facebook Messenger, "Hi Amy, I received your letter to my brother, Charles, and if what you say is true, I'm your uncle, Jerry."

So much for all the warning labels; the cat is out of the bag—or envelope. I immediately respond, "It's definitely true. Nice to meet you, Uncle Jerry."

"I'd like to call you. Would that be okay?" is Jerry's response.

"Yes, please!" And I give him my phone number.

Immediately, the phone rings, and I answer, "Hello, this is Amy."

"Hi Amy, this is your Uncle Jerry."

"Hi, Uncle Jerry. I hope you believe what I told you is true." I feel an overwhelming need to know that he believes me.

"I believe you," he says, and relief floods over me. We talk for a few minutes, and then Jerry asks if he and his wife,

Anne, can come to my house and meet me. I assume this is a way for him to check me out before he will, hopefully, share the news with his brother.

A couple of weeks later, they make the four-hour drive to meet me. When they pull into our driveway, I wave to them from the porch, squinting to see Jerry's face through the tinted glass. Jerry is thirteen years younger than my birth father, which makes him only ten years older than me. His hair and beard are white and he bears a striking resemblance to Santa Claus wearing a cowboy hat. I feel like I know them since I've stalked their photos on Facebook for weeks.

We hug when they get out of the truck, and Jerry gets a large box of old family photos out of the back of his truck. Story hour turns into story "many" hours as we sit in the living room looking through those photos. Jerry tells stories to go along with many of them, and I'm disappointed to learn that most of my birth father's photos perished in a fire before Jerry was born. I long to hear childhood stories about Charlie, which is how I now refer to my birth father because it seems everyone in the family does. Charlie joined the Air Force when Jerry was just a young boy. Too many years separate them, and the stories I imagined about two boys growing up together simply don't exist. I learn that Charlie married just a couple years after I was born and had two more children, a son and a daughter. When that marriage ended, he married the woman he is currently married to and helped raise her daughter, who I'm told will love having me as a sister.

I pore over the images of relatives I never knew I had. I'm fascinated to hear stories about my grandma Gilda, who was born in 1912, coincidently the same year as my mom. I see myself in some of Gilda's facial features and wish I could have met her. I'm told she lived a hard life after her husband, my grandfather, died at the age of forty, leaving her with six children to raise by herself. She passed away at ninety-one, and I take some comfort that I have a grandmother who lived a long life and whose mind remained sharp until the end.

As their visit comes to an end and they are ready to leave, Uncle Jerry delivers a parting blow, "I'm not sure I want to share the news of you with Charlie. His health is not good, and I worry about him. I'll have to think about it."

His words knock the wind out of me, leaving me speechless though my brain is screaming, "*Whaaaaaat? How can you keep this from him? What happened? Did I fail the test?"* But then another voice interrupts in my head (How many voices are in there anyway?), "*Maybe this is for the best. Maybe this is all you need to know."*

The next day, Jerry calls, "I've talked to Crystal, Charlie's stepdaughter, and I'm sending her the letter so she can take it to him. Anne said I really have no right to keep this information from him, and she's right." I'm thrilled! Thank You, Jesus (and thank you, Aunt Anne and Uncle Jerry)! Just a week later, I receive *THE* call.

"Hello, is this Amy?" The voice sounds just like Uncle Jerry, but the phone number on the caller ID is wrong, and I know instantly that this is my birth father.

"Yes, it is." My poor heart is racing again.

"Hi, Amy, this is your dad. I'm really sorry it took so long for you to find me."

"Hi, Dad!" We chat for about ten minutes as he tells me a little about his childhood and ends the call by saying he's going to be visiting Jerry in a month and would love it if I would come there to meet him. And with that, the plan is set. I'm going to meet my birth father!

I hang up the phone with only one regret. I've done it again. I called him "Dad," a name reserved for only one until now.

It's a Girl!

TJ and I make the drive to Uncle Jerry's house and stand at the front door. The now familiar combination of excitement and nerves runs through me as I ring the doorbell. A dog barks, and I hear voices inside as TJ captures the moment on my phone. It seems to take forever for the door to open, but when it does, I see my birth father, Charlie, standing tall and handsome with silver hair and bright blue eyes. He opens his arms wide, and I go to him. We embrace in a long hug as he laughs, "It took you long enough to find me!"

"I know!" I say with eyes closed. Every part of my face is smiling.

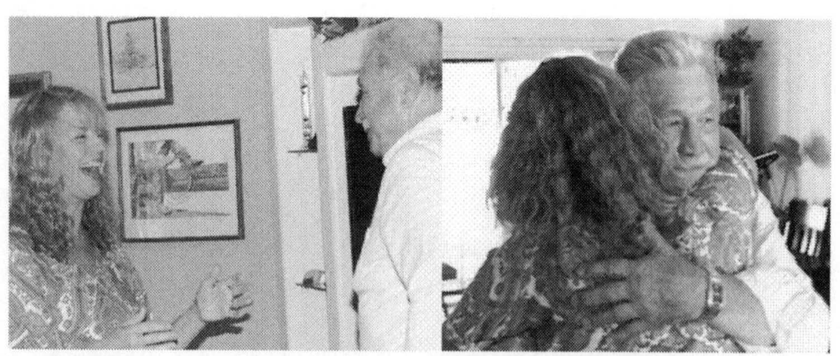

The hug ends, and he steadies himself against the wall. Smiling, he asks, "Why didn't your mother tell somebody? Here's the sad part: her cousin, who introduced me to her, knows where I've been the entire time. All she would have had to do was ask him."

"Is that right?" I'm taken aback at how fast we get into that conversation and wonder, could it have been that simple? Jean can no longer answer that question, but does it even matter? "Well, her memory never was that good, and she has Alzheimer's now," I tell him.

"I do that to girls," he says, and we all laugh. The awkward moment is instantly forgotten.

TJ hands Charlie a cigar wrapped in a pink "It's a girl" band, and we sit down as Charlie begins to tell his version of how I came to be.

"I remember the day I met your mom. See, I had this convertible and my friend, your mom's cousin, wanted me to drive him to Superior for a graduation party for his cousin. That would be your mom's sister. Anyway, Superior was about an hour away from where I lived, and I really didn't want to go, so I kept telling him no, but he just wouldn't let up. I think he really just wanted to ride in that convertible. When he told me there would be lots of good food and pretty girls there, I figured I really had nothing better to do. When we got there, he introduced me to your mom. She was really pretty, but I have to tell you, I didn't know she was married, or I would never have given her the time of day. I've never been that kind of guy, you know what I mean?"

I nod, and he continues. "When my friend and I were driving home after the party, he asked me if I knew Jean was married. I accused him of joking with me. I just couldn't believe it."

I sit transfixed by the story and have to make sure my mouth's not hanging open. I don't really know how to respond, so I just keep nodding my head like one of those bobblehead dogs that people used to put on their car dash.

He continues, "About a year later, something makes me think about Jean, and I ask her cousin how she's doing. I casually ask him if she's had any more kids. He said he didn't think so but didn't know for sure. I guess I never really thought about it after that."

He doesn't mention the story that Jean told me, that she went to see him to tell him she was pregnant. Could that be why he asked her cousin if she'd had any more babies? I never tell him the story Jean told me. It's just another thing that doesn't seem to matter anymore.

I hear story after story that brings some insight into the person he is and was. He and Jerry laugh as they recount stories of the bar fights Charlie could never walk away from, and they both talk lovingly about their mother, Gilda.

When I pull out the first of the childhood photo albums I've brought with me, I expect to point out what some photos represent as Charlie examines each one like Jean did.

Instead, he thumbs through the pages quickly, only glancing at the photos. Sometimes he doesn't even look at the pages as he turns them while telling more stories about his life. I stop hearing the words he's saying when this happens, feeling hurt by his apparent lack of interest in my childhood. All I can hear are the thoughts in my head, and I once again over-analyze the situation. *Why isn't he interested in my childhood? Could this just be the difference between a man and a woman, or a father and a mother, or just the difference in people in general? Or, just maybe, it's because he's eighty years old.* Whatever the reason, I stop trying to point out anything in my photos.

Closing the cover of the first album, he hands it to me and I put it back in the box with the two others I've brought, ending the Life of Amy photo tour. He doesn't ask me about the other albums clearly visible in the box beside me. In fact, he doesn't ask me anything about my childhood at all. He enjoys sharing his stories though, and I decide I'm okay with that. It is, after all, what I've always wanted—to know about my birth father and the family who came with him and before him.

The next day, we have a family barbecue, and I meet two more cousins, including Uncle Jerry's daughter, who actually resembles my youngest daughter. Our visit ends with us promising to visit Charlie in a month for his eighty-first birthday.

Slipping Away

Jean's memory continues to fade, and when my brother Danny realizes he can no longer care for her in his home, he moves her into an assisted living facility. Visiting her is difficult for me in more ways than one, the first being that I now live in the mountains, 180 miles away from her. It's horrible to watch Jean's mind slip away, which only heightens my fear of the disease that two successive generations have now bestowed upon me, like some demonic gift that keeps on giving, and that nightmare train is heading my way. "All aboard!" There's no way to sugarcoat that seeing Jean feels like a preview of my future, and I'm in full self-preservation mode by avoiding contact with it.

I know this is selfish, but one thing makes it a little easier. The mother-daughter bond that my mom and I shared is not there with Jean. I now believe that parental bond results from raising a child and the experiences shared. I've had that love. I know what it feels like. I don't think blood has anything to do with it. Love is not genetic. I don't think you love someone just because you're related to them, but if that's true, how do I explain my overwhelming love for my daughters from the moment they were born? It was not a love born of shared experience at all. I spend far too much time analyzing the situation and never come to a full understanding of why, after all these years, Jean and I have never been more than friends.

Regardless, I make the 360-mile round trip to visit Jean at the assisted living center when possible. After finding my birth father, I'm excited to share this information with her. I decide to do it in person, hoping enough of her memory remains so she'll understand and enjoy hearing all the stories about him. I call to tell her I'm coming and will pick her up at 11:30 to take her for lunch. She sounds happy about it.

When I arrive, I find her at a table in the dining room with some of the other women living there. I'd love to call them her friends, but they're not. Jean still doesn't like socializing and keeps to herself most of the time.

I walk up to the table. "Hi, Mom," I say, bending over to hug her.

"You're late. I didn't think you were coming," she exclaims loudly.

"I told you I'd pick you up at 11:30. I'm actually early."

"No, you're late," she insists. All movement seems to have stopped in the dining room. *Is everyone looking at us? Do they always keep it so hot in here?*

"Okay, well, you haven't eaten yet, so do you want to go out for lunch?" I say, winking at the little lady in pink sitting next to her.

"You should go, Jean," the pink lady says.

"Okay," Jean says, standing. I take her hand and help her walk to the lobby. I'm taken aback by her physical decline since I last saw her a couple of months ago, and I remember the first time she took my hand when I found her thirty-two years ago.

I lead her to a bench in the foyer, where I sit her down and tell her, "Wait here; I'll go get the car." There's no way she can walk that far, especially in the heat. I return, driving up to the front door, and run back inside the building to retrieve her, leaving the car running to cool it, but Jean's gone. I return to the car, turn it off, grab my purse, and rush back to the dining room. She's not there.

"Have you seen my mom?" I ask the pink lady.

"No, honey, I haven't. Wasn't she with you?"

"I left her in the lobby while I went to get the car," I explain.

"Well, maybe she went to the ladies' room. It's just down that hallway."

I enter the restroom, where two stall doors are closed. "Mom?"

"Yes," two voices respond. Great. I recognize neither.

"Jean?" I ask again, bending over to see if I can recognize her feet, just as I hear the toilet flush. Jean steps out of the stall and starts towards the door.

"Here, let's wash your hands," I say, walking to the sink.

"I didn't pee on my hands," she states matter-of-factly as she exits.

Driving to the restaurant, Jean says, "I'm not very hungry. I need some new underpants."

"Okay, well, I'm hungry. So let's go to the restaurant, and you can have something to drink if you're still not hungry when we get there, okay? And then we'll stop at the store on the way home."

"Okay."

Once seated at our table, Jean decides she's hungry after all, and we order. While we wait for our food, I say, "Guess what? I found my birth father!"

"Who?"

"My birth father. You remember? Charles Neal?"

"Oh. I don't think I know him. It's really cold in here."

The end. Her mind can no longer engage in this revelation of mine, and in that moment, I ponder God's timing, marveling at the bittersweet irony of it all. How He led me to my birth father just as my birth mother can barely remember who I am.

I decide to let the birth father topic drop and pull some photos I've found on ancestry.com out of my purse. "Look at this photo I found." I say, pointing to each person in the shot,

"See, this is your mom from when she was young. Look here. That's you, your brother, and your sister when you were all little."

She takes the photo from me and draws it closer to her eyes. "That's my mom?" she asks.

"Yes, it is."

"My poor mom. My dad left her for another woman, and she had to care for us three kids all by herself."

"Really? Tell me about it." I've heard the story before, but I'm hoping to have something—anything to talk about.

"Our food's here," is her response.

And that's the end of her story. After a couple of bites of her burger, she says, "It's too cold in here. Can we leave?"

I get our lunches put into to-go boxes and start our slow walk back to the car. She holds onto my arm as I carry our two purses and our lunches. Then suddenly, she's going down. Like slow motion, she crumples onto the hot pavement. I drop the purses and the lunches and struggle to lift her off the hot pavement before her skin burns. When she's finally upright, I brush her off and check her for any injuries, and I'm thankful there aren't any. I get her buckled up in the car, turn on the air conditioning, and retrieve our lunches and purses that are still in a heap on the ground.

Back in the car, I ask, "Do you have a special store where you'd like to buy your underpants?"

"I don't need underpants. I want to go home."

I'm no longer shocked by anything that comes out of her mouth. "Okay." I better get her home. She may forget who I am at any minute and try to get out of the car. I hate this disease.

When we enter her apartment, she tells me, "I don't like it here. Someone stole my phone."

"Really? Are you sure? Who do you think did that?"

"I don't know."

"Well, I'll tell Danny so he can look into it, okay?"

"Danny is the one who takes care of me," she says, a statement, not a question.

"Yes, Mom, Danny is your son, and he takes care of you." There is no response to this. "Do you want to eat our lunches at the table?"

"No, I'm not hungry."

I decide I'm really not hungry either. I put both lunches in the refrigerator as she walks over to the TV, turns it on, sits in her recliner, and disappears into another world. When I hear a phone ringing, I follow the sound to her linen closet, where I find her phone behind a stack of towels.

"Mom, look, I found your phone! Nobody stole it. Isn't that great?" I hold it out to her, but she's lost in TV Land, so I lay it beside her on the end table. I have to go. I can't bear any of this.

"Well, I'm going to go home now, Mom. I have a long drive ahead of me. Do you have everything you need? Is there anything I can get you?" She doesn't take her eyes off the TV, so I move between her and the TV and wave my arms around to get her attention.

"Mom, I found your phone and laid it right there beside you, okay? Your lunch is in the refrigerator. I'm going to go home now," I say, speaking louder and more slowly than I probably need to.

"Okay."

"Do you need anything?"

"No, I'm fine."

If only that were true.

"I love you," I say and kiss her cheek.

Nothing.

I walk to the door, looking back to see that she's been swallowed up by her TV show once again. I close the door behind me, wondering if she'll remember I was here or if she'll even remember me again. The thought lingers as I walk down the corridor, feeling the ache of losing her even before she's truly gone.

Surreality

Two days before we're scheduled to visit Charlie for his eighty-first birthday, and just a month after I met him, he suffers a heart attack. I pray I won't lose him so soon after finding him. TJ and I make the trip as planned and spend two days sitting by his bed at the hospital, often accompanied by his stepdaughter, Crystal, who is a sweetheart and obviously loves Charlie, who she calls dad because he has been every bit of a dad to her.

On the last day of our visit, the doctor comes in to present treatment options while TJ and I sit there beside his hospital bed. When the doctor asks if I'm family, the question catches me off guard. The lag time of my response is palpable. "Yes," I finally respond. How do I tell him I've just stepped into this family like a minute ago?

I become increasingly uncomfortable as the doctor lays out treatment options. The doctor probably knows the patient better than I do, and I'm far from qualified to offer any opinion on treatment. I listen and nod, and if wishes could come true, Crystal would walk into this room right this minute. I finally tell the doctor, "I'm just here visiting, but his other daughter Crystal lives near him and will be here shortly. She'll be the point person for his care, and I will share that information with her."

The doctor's face changes when he realizes I'm one of "those" daughters. You know, a daughter in name only, who is never around when a parent really needs her? That's never been me, and I shrink in my chair. It becomes clear that it doesn't matter. Charlie doesn't need anyone to speak for him. He's thrown off the sheet and declared, "I'm ready to go home. Get me out of here." No more discussion is needed, and in this moment, I see where I got this strong and sometimes uncompromising will of mine.

After he's discharged, I push him in a wheelchair to the hospital pharmacy, and he hands me his wallet so I can pick up his prescriptions. The whole thing feels surreal. TJ brings the car to the front of the hospital, and we're soon on the road for the hour-long drive to Charlie's house. While TJ and Charlie enjoy a conversation in the front seat, I sit quietly in the back, marveling at God. Less than a year ago, I didn't even know for sure who my birth father was,` and now I'm riding down the road studying the back of his head.

Dust in the Sunlight

TJ accompanies me for support the next time I visit Jean. Driving from our mountain home, we pass through Superior as we usually do.

"Where's the smokestack?" I ask, scanning the spot where that familiar landmark stood for over ninety-four years and served as an awkward reminder of where I began, literally.

"Wow, they must have torn it down," he says, stating the obvious.

Indeed, they have. The 293-foot monument marking the spot of my conception is no more. All the dots in my life have been connected, so it seems appropriate somehow that it's gone.

We stop at a grocery store to pick up some flowers in a vase to take to Jean. Arriving at the assisted living complex where I last visited her, I'm informed they have transferred her to the memory care facility next door. We walk across the parking lot and sign in, and an attendant escorts us to Jean's room. We walk past rooms that are like hospital rooms instead of the apartment she had been living in, and most of the doors are closed. We pass a large room where several residents gather around a TV that's playing an old black-and-white western. Some residents are talking to no one in particular with random sentences that have nothing to do with the world around them. One woman is standing in the corner facing the wall. It's a "*One Flew Over the Cuckoo's Nest*" theatrical production, and none of these characters have to rehearse. I close my eyes for a few seconds as I walk. "God, give me strength."

The attendant leads us to the end of the hall and unlocks the door to Jean's room. "Why is her door locked?" I ask.

"It's for her safety," he tells me, then says loudly as he opens the door, "Hi, Jean. You've got company." Then he turns and leaves us alone with her.

Jean makes no response. In fact, I can't even tell if she knows anyone has entered her room. It's 1:30 in the afternoon, and she's lying in bed in her nightgown. I'm shocked to see how thin she is, a shell of who she was, lying there watching static on the TV. The once beautiful woman who turned heads when she entered a room and who took such great care to look her best is gone.

My mind flashes to all the diets we've been on together as we tried in vain to attain the supermodel target weight she now appears to have achieved—weird thought to have in this moment. I break the silence, "Hi, Mom! What are you doing in your nightgown in the middle of the day?" My voice sounds too loud and too chipper, like I'm trying way too hard — because I am.

"Who are you?" She asks and my heart sinks as the moment I've dreaded arrives. She no longer knows who I am.."

"It's me, Amy." Not a grain of recognition. "Your daughter?"

"You are? Well, isn't that nice."

Then her voice changes. "And who are you? Aren't you handsome."

Is that her flirty voice?

"Mom, you remember TJ, my husband, right?"

"Well, hello, TJ."

Yes, definitely her flirty voice.

"Hi, Jean," TJ says, winking at me. A wink I hope he never has to use if my mind evaporates.

I'm still standing in the doorway, paralyzed and holding the vase of flowers. "We brought you some flowers, Mom. Aren't they pretty?"

No response.

"I'll put them on this table by the TV so you can see them."

Still nothing. I go to her and kiss her cheek. She smells sour.

"And who are you?" she asks again.

"I'm your daughter, Amy." Nothing.

Time slows as I try to figure out what to do from here. I've always dreaded small talk, and it doesn't get much smaller than this. Every piece of me wants to run out of this room, get in the car, and drive home without looking back.

Then she speaks, still looking at TJ, "What's your name?" Her flirty voice again. Somebody, please wake me.

"It's TJ." He looks at me and opens his eyes wide, like, "Now what?"

"Are you married?" she asks.

TJ smiles, and I interrupt this mortifying line of questioning."So, Mom, how are you feeling? I sit on the side of her bed. I don't know what else to say, but I have to turn off this awkward flirting. I have to keep her from embarrassing herself, though I know that embarrassment is not likely a feeling in her repertoire anymore.

"They hit me, you know. I really don't like it here."

"Who hits you, Mom?"

"Everyone. All the time."

Surely this is the disease talking. "Where did they hit you?"

"Can you take me with you?"

"Can you show me where they hit you?" I ask, trying to determine if what she tells me is real or all in her mind. I've seen news stories about stuff like that happening.

As I check her back, arms, and legs for any signs of abuse and see none, she asks, "Who hit me?"

"No one, Mom. Next time we come, how about we take you for a ride? Maybe we can take you to church for Easter. Would you like that?"

"Yes."

"Okay, we'll plan that." I know we can never take her out of this place, and I hate that I'm lying to her. I search for something else to say.

"Why do you have static on your TV? Can I turn something on for you?" I ask, walking over to the TV and changing the channel to a game show because it sounds loud, happy, and normal in this world where nothing feels normal. But she's not watching. Even the TV can't capture her attention anymore. Her eyes are suddenly vacant, like what little is left of her has stepped away and her eyes are simply placeholders. Her face is now turned toward the window.

"Is there anything I can get you, Mom? Something to eat? Are you thirsty?" Nothing. I feel the tears coming. I can't let them start, or they may not stop,

"Okay, Mom. Well, it's time for us to go." We've only been there a few minutes, but I can't see how this visit is doing either of us any good. I bend over and kiss her cheek again, but her eyes don't see me.

"I love you, Mom," I say, expecting more of nothing as we walk to the door. But then I hear, "I love you, too."

I turn to see the woman who gave me life, watching dust float in the sunlight. My heart knows this is the last time I will ever see her, but I will never forget this memory of her.

It will haunt me until the day I die or until I start watching static on the TV and dust floating in the sunlight.

As I close the door behind us, she says, “Please take me with you." I can’t hold back the tears and TJ takes my hand. We let the attendant know we’re leaving so he can lock her in again, and we walk silently to the car. If a moment ever deserved a sad soundtrack, this is it.

TJ breaks the silence. “You know we can never take her for a ride or to church, right?”

“I know.”

“Are you okay?”

“I’m okay. It’s just so sad.”

“I don’t think she knows what’s going on, so we can probably be thankful for that.”

“I hope that’s true." We ride in silence until I dare to speak my fear out loud. “Am I going to end up like that?”

“You won’t.” Poor TJ, he doesn’t understand the button he’s just pressed.

“How can you know that? First Grandma Mae and now Jean and I’ve had just about everything Jean has ever had medically. I can’t picture a more horrible way to die, at least for the family. Promise you’ll put me away somewhere or just keep me sedated if this happens to me. Maybe just drop me off in the middle of the desert so the coyotes will eat me —whatever—anything so no one I love has to deal with that.” I realize I’m spiraling here.

"Baby, stop, just stop. I'll always take care of you." TJ is finally able to get a word in.

"But I don't want you to have to take care of me," I say, staring out the passenger window and seeing nothing. "I want to remember Jean, how she was, but it's going to be hard getting this final version of her out of my head." And that much will prove to be true.

Two days after Jean is placed in hospice care in August 2017, my phone rings and I see Danny's number come up on my caller ID. I know before I even answer that Jean has died. He tells me her passing was peaceful. Alzheimer's took her body six years after it took her mind. I thank Danny for letting me know. It will be the last words we share. The one who connected us is gone.

I have no tears at her passing. I shed those tears when the disease stole the essence of who she was because that's really when she died. So, where one would expect sadness, instead, I feel thankful that she's no longer trapped in the shell that held her soul captive. I won't even say the comforting words we always say, that she's at peace because I know what she's feeling now is greater than peace. She's jumping for joy in the presence of Jesus, the One she loved more than anything. The One she had always longed to be with.

And Then There Were None

2019—My birth father died today, three years after our first meeting and just a month after his eighty-fourth birthday, which, coincidently, is the same age my dad was when he died.

I visited Charlie for his eighty-third birthday, and we texted and spoke on the phone occasionally, although he admitted he wasn't much of a talk-on-the-phone kind of guy. Several heart attacks would follow that first one as his health declined. He was in hospice care at the end, so his passing isn't a surprise when I receive the call. I'm thankful that he and the rest of the family welcomed me into their lives and that God gave us the time we had.

At his passing, I feel my adoption journey has come full circle. The four people on Earth who contributed to my existence have passed on. Two who gave me life and two who gave me so much to live for. Each one leaving behind a beautiful mark of their presence on my life.

It's a story with an awkward beginning and a beautiful ending—a tale of a boy who met a girl at a party he didn't want to go to and their not-so-great decision that resulted in my oh-so-great beating heart. The girl who loved me enough to give me away—and the parents who loved me enough to give a little of me back. What an incredible gift I've been given.

So What's Next?

2021—Today we left our beloved mountain home in Arizona, saying goodbye to family, friends, church family, and the community we love as we set out for our next adventure in Kentucky.

I can't explain this cross-country move that still makes little sense to us. Why, at this point in our lives, would we leave the place we've been so blessed to call home? And why would a tiny town in the Middle of Nowhere, Kentucky, a place we've never been, be our destination? All I can say is that even after praying about it (and secretly hoping the Lord would bring me to my senses and tell me to stay put), the overwhelming feeling that we were supposed to move to Kentucky grew to the point I began looking at Kentucky homes for sale online. And just like that, I found "the house," the farmhouse that has lived in my heart for so long, like my heart knew before I did that I would eventually live there. The white farmhouse with the black shutters and porch swing is almost identical to the framed painting that's hung on my wall for over twenty-five years. The one that whenever I'm asked about it, I say, "It's the house my heart has always wanted to live in."

When I show the listing to TJ, he says, "Let's do it." That's how TJ rolls. I, on the other hand, start listing the many reasons this idea is insane. The first is that we're in Arizona, it's in Kentucky, and houses are selling in minutes, not months. The following day, I can't stop thinking about the house, so I walk across the street to show the listing to my neighbor. By the time I knock on her door, I've just about talked myself out of doing anything with this house in Kentucky, but I show her the photos anyway and then give her my list of reasons it isn't likely to happen.

Then she says, "You know that if God wants you to move to Kentucky, and if this is the house He's placed on your heart, then it's already yours. If you're not even going to try, how will you ever know?" And she's right.

With a renewed sense of excitement, I hurry home to tell TJ. We call the listing agent, who informs us she already has an offer on the house (well, of course, she does) and will present it to the sellers in four hours. Then, throwing all logic and reason to the wind, we tell her we would also like to write an offer.

That evening, we receive the call, "The sellers have accepted your offer, and the house is yours!" She continues, "By the way, both offers were virtually identical, and I advised the sellers to counter both offers, but they said they felt God wanted you to have their house. They feel so strongly about it; they won't even let me keep the listing active for backup offers." There's God again.

So here we are, living in the Middle of Nowhere, Kentucky, with cows as our only neighbors but closer to Jesus than we've ever been. God had not only prepared a home for us but also had our church family already in place. Walking into our new church felt like coming home. We can't wait to see what God has in store for us next.

So how do we explain these things of God? I don't know that we can fully understand His ways, but after this journey, I know beyond a shadow of a doubt that our God is bigger than doubt, bigger than fear and that He leads us right where He wants us if we'll listen for His voice and trust Him.

The Big Question

Finding my birth parents answered many of my questions, yet didn't fully resolve the one that started it all, "Who am I?"

The nature vs. nurture debate always comes to mind. On the one hand, the nature side tells us we're born with a unique set of genes that shape our physical traits and potentially even our tendencies, handed down through generations like a family heirloom or, depending on the circumstances, a family curse. Meeting my birth parents revealed traits in me, for better or worse, that echo theirs—including similar physical characteristics. But this journey has taught me that my identity isn't confined to my gene pool.

Then there's the nurture side of the equation. Our upbringing molds our habits, preferences, and values. Given how many of my mannerisms, values, and traditions align with those of my parents who adopted me, I've always leaned toward this perspective.

But is that all we are? A bundle of traits wrapped in skin? While they may influence our journey, I don't believe they define our essence or who we really are.

Adopted—a powerful word that defined me my entire life, and rightly so. Adoption changed my destiny, and my story cannot be told without it. Yet there's an even more profound adoption that speaks to the core of who I really am: my adoption into the family of God through faith in Christ.

John 1:12-13 says, *"Yet to all who did receive him, to those who believed in his name, he gave the right to become children of God—children born not of natural descent, nor of human decision or a husband's will, but born of God."* It is this adoption that changes everything, including our eternal destiny, which is the most important story of all.

So, who am I? I am a child of God, called to live a "life adopted" with all the promise that it holds. As I let go of the traits and tendencies that hold me back and draw closer to Him, I discover the incredible plan He designed just for me and the miraculous peace that a relationship with Him brings.

Once upon a time, all I wanted was to fit in with everyone around me, but my heart has changed since I began walking with Jesus. Now, I just want to be more like Him.

I've been called to live a life adopted, and so have you.

The Gift of Hindsight

I've discovered many things as I dusted off my memories, many of which had lain undisturbed for years in the bog of a cluttered mind. Reflection is an excellent tool for seeing things more clearly, where we've been and how we got to where we are. From here, I can see God's miracles where all my coincidences used to be. The circumstances that all came together were not just a lucky accident.

I understand now that my birth mother did not reject me. It was she who saved me. I wasn't a mistake because no child ever is. The genesis of a beating heart has no bearing on its legitimacy, value, or purpose.

The Bible says God is the Potter, and we are the clay. I'm thankful for that because I've still got plenty of things that need to be reshaped. For one, I'm still pretty good at building walls —big, ugly, impenetrable walls. Smooth walls that can't be scaled, and some with a bit of barbed wire on top for extra measure. Walls constructed from bricks of hurt and fear held together with mortar of pride. I've grown quite attached to my walls, even though I know they're not a part of God's blueprint for my life. But as God reveals how and why they're messing with His plan, they begin to come down, brick by brick. There aren't as many now, and maybe someday I'll have my "Jericho" moment, and they'll all come tumbling down. Scary thought, but one I'm praying for. How much more could God accomplish through me if I wasn't hiding behind those walls? This book is another step towards that. It's hard to hide when you put a book about your life and innermost thoughts on public display. But when God says, "Tell your story," you do.

The rejection complex that once loomed large in my life now feels like a faint echo of its former self. When it flares up today, I remind myself of the One who, though sinless, was scorned by the world. He paid the ultimate price for my sins, enduring a brutal death on a cross so I could be forgiven. Jesus gave everything, yet He's still being rejected by many He came to save. Amidst a raging sea, He stands in the lifeboat, with arms reaching out, while countless people choose to be swept away by the waves. His heart must ache, knowing what awaits those who turn away from Him. That's the only rejection truly worthy of my tears.

Epilogue

It has taken me seven years to complete the task God asked me to do—embarrassingly too long. But somehow, even that number shows me God's hand in the whole thing. Seven, the number signifying completion, appears more than 700 times in the Bible. Completion. How can I not see Him in that? What I thought of as dragging my feet may have had a purpose. My faith has grown significantly over that time as I've spent time with the Lord and time in my memories. I see many things more clearly today than when I started this journey.

That said, I know another element was involved with the delay. Something that was not of God—the whispers of doubt and criticism in my head never stopped from the moment I began writing until I submitted it for publishing. I finally recognize that the enemy will do everything he can to keep us from doing what God wants us to do. He knows our weaknesses and was skilled at throwing rocks at my confidence, using only a whisper.

Then, just when I thought I had finished editing my book for the last time, an email pops up in my inbox with the subject line blaring, "The Do's and Don'ts of Writing." First, let me say I have no idea why this email came to me and on the day I thought my book was finally finished, of all days. I've not received a single email with writing tips before this one showed up. I wince when I see it, wondering if it's from God or the devil. So, like a builder who takes a first look at the house plans the day he's finished building the house, I open the email and read.

Rule #1, "Know your target audience."

Who is my target audience? Do I even have one? When I started this journey, I would have said that my target audience was anyone touched by adoption. But now it seems broader, and I ask myself, have I gone too far, included too much, lost my focus?

My elation at completing the task God has given me turns to panic, and I end up disemboweling all that I've written, pulling out the adoption story so it can stand alone. It's painstaking, but there it is, and now my story has a target audience. But when I look at the words left lying on the cutting room floor like frayed threads, I realize my story can't be told without them. Those discarded threads must be woven together with my adoption story to create the tapestry that is my life.

Romans 8:28 says, "*And we know that in all things God works for the good of those who love him, who have been called according to his purpose."* So, *r*egardless of who or what led to the seven-year delay in completing this book, I know that God orchestrated it for a greater purpose. His purpose.

So I weave all the frayed threads back together; the dark, the light, the beautiful, and the ugly, and I'll leave it to God to decide who my target audience is. If you've made it this far, Dear Reader, you're it.

May my story encourage you to open your eyes and see God in your life. See the story that He's written just for you. See His miracles where your coincidences used to be. And when you see, remember this: your story is not just for you; it's for Him. So don't keep it a secret. Tell your story. Share what God has done in your life.

God has a plan for every heartbeat, and every heartbeat has a story to tell. Thank you for letting me tell you mine.

And one more thing . . . or two

This earthly life is nothing but a blink when compared to eternity. What truly matters at the end of this life on earth is where we'll spend forever. Our bodies will die, but our souls will live on. So, here's the bottom line: Jesus Christ is the Son of God, heaven and hell are real, and so is the devil—who will do everything he can to keep you away from Jesus. Whether you believe these things or not doesn't change the truth.

If you were to die tomorrow, do you know where you're going? By accepting Christ's gift of salvation—a gift that can't be earned, but must be accepted—you can have peace in knowing where you will spend eternity. Don't turn your back on the greatest gift ever given. Jesus is calling. Please don't wait until it's too late to accept His call.

"For God so loved the world that he gave his one and only Son, that whoever believes in him shall not perish but have eternal life. For God did not send his Son into the world to condemn the world, but to save the world through him. Whoever believes in him is not condemned, but whoever does not believe stands condemned already because they have not believed in the name of God's one and only Son."

John 3:16-18

four generations

Reflecting on this photo of my birth mother, my daughter, my granddaughter, and me, I'm reminded of the weight of her decision and how precious her choice was. One single selfless decision that saved not just one life but generations. My heart overflows with gratitude that words can't fully capture.

Over the seven years that I was writing this book, more than half a Billion babies have lost their lives through abortion. Each one, a fleeting life that never had the chance to blossom. with dreams that were extinguished before they could even flicker.

If they could have spoken to the one who carried them, I believe these are the words they would say—

I am

Here. Created in an instant. Like a spark.
Alive and perfectly contained.
Every cell holding the truth of who I am and who I will be.

I am

Alive and growing with beating heart
Just as God knew I would be
From the beginning of time.

I am

Human with unique DNA.
No one like me has ever existed.
No one like me will ever exist again.

If only

I could tell you the plans God has for me
And for the ones who will come from me.

If only

I could tell you we're all here
And you're the only one who can save us.

If only

I could tell you the choice you're making
Is not just for you, it's for all of us.

If only

I could tell you.
If only someone would.

~Amy R. Jones

Acknowledgments

Thank you, TJ, for your never-ending encouragement and leaving me undisturbed (most of the time) to write; for listening when I wanted you to and for offering advice when I needed it but told you I didn't; and for your patience when you asked if you could read some of what I'd written and I always said "No." Thank you for loving me so deeply and for loving Jesus even more. I love you.

To everyone who has asked, "When's your book gonna be done?" (You know who you are.) Thank you for letting God use you to keep me on track. It was often just the nudge I needed.

Thank You, Jesus, for loving me so much that you died for me. May I never lose the wonder of Your presence in my life as I continue to share all You've done. Thank You, God, for your endless mercy and grace as I stumbled through this task You set before me. The story You asked me to tell is finished, but the journey isn't over. Whatever you have for me next, Lord, I'm ready. Send me.

I have been crucified with Christ and I no longer live, but Christ lives in me. The life I now live in the body, I live by faith in the Son of God, who loved me and gave himself for me. *Galatians 2:20*

Made in the USA
Middletown, DE
09 September 2024